"Brant Hansen manages to be both [   ] serious. *The Men We Need* is a blas[   ] edly earnest for men to be exactly what God has created us to be and what the world is waiting to see."

Kyle Idleman, bestselling author of *Not a Fan*
and *One at a Time*

"This is not only the book every man needs, it's also one every woman should read. In a time when everyone is asking, 'What does it really mean to be a man?' Brant Hansen gives a compelling, insightful, and deeply helpful response. I read this book in one sitting, and it made me nod, laugh out loud, and want to share it with every man and woman I know."

Holley Gerth, *Wall Street Journal* bestselling author
of *The Powerful Purpose of Introverts*

"Brant Hansen has done it again—this time with a funny, punchy book on manhood. Full of hard-won wisdom and simple, biblical truths applied across the spectrum of the masculine experience, *The Men We Need* is the book we need for our confused cultural moment."

Jared C. Wilson, assistant professor of pastoral ministry
and author in residence at Midwestern Seminary;
author of *Love Me Anyway*

"Brant Hansen is a marvel in this modern world. Rarely do I meet someone with a voice that is equally insightful, comedic, and piercing. I invite you to dive in and experience Brant's kingdom-centered, upside-down perspective."

Mike Donehey, recording artist;
author of *Finding God's Life for My Will*

"Read this book and start being awesome. We women are rooting for you."

Lisa Anderson, director of Boundless.org;
author of *The Dating Manifesto*

"Brant gives words to feelings we have and purpose that we never considered. I was a young man during an era when Christian masculinity was defined by growing a beard and being one with the wild. Trouble was, I had little wild and only heart. And I still can't grow a beard. This book is written for me and my boys. It's probably written for you and your boys as well. It's for those of us who love Jesus and are discovering that protecting the vulnerable, selflessly loving our family, and showing up for the hurting are evidence of being a man of God. Our world will be a more redemptive place as you rise to the challenge. We all hope you will!"

Justin Narducci, president/CEO of CURE
International Children's Hospitals

"In a time of chaos, confusion, and even despair, when women and children around the world are as at risk as ever, Brant Hansen's brilliant, insightful, funny, and convicting book is not only a breath of sane biblical reason but a balm to the internet-addled soul. The vision of masculinity he sets forth is within the grasp of any man at any stage of life, and his practical and gracious wisdom is enlivening. I'm planning to read the book out loud to both my sons, just as soon as I throw their Xbox into the river."

Anne Kennedy, author of *Nailed It: 365 Readings
for Angry or Worn-Out People*

"Our societies send very confusing messages on what it means to be a man. Brant turns that all on its head. In his usual winsome style, he gives us a book that is relatable, convicting, and timeless. I'm fortunate enough to know Brant and to have been personally challenged by him to be the man I was designed to be. Those who benefit? My wife, my children, my community, and my colleagues. I'm excited others are now getting this challenge too. Whether you are in your teens or in those outer years, this book offers course corrections to help us be the manliest of men."

Derek Johnson, head of US Operations & Strategy,
International Justice Mission

"Employing his singular wit, Brant graciously challenges men to become what our families and our world need us to be—protectors and defenders. I especially recommend this book as a call to action for young men."

Benjamin C. Warf, MD, professor of neurosurgery
at Harvard Medical School

"*The Men We Need* is perfectly titled. Because the world *is* desperate for the men Brant describes. This book gives men a vision for what masculinity really can be: the kind that protects and brings life to everyone around. And somehow Brant manages to be both deeply serious and deeply funny. Once again he hit it out of the park."

Bill Yeargin, CEO, Correct Craft, Inc.

"As a marriage and women's counselor, I'm deeply aware of the confusion, brokenness, purposelessness, and ongoing sense of failure many men live with. Yet I'm equally aware of the distortions, the settling, and the 'I guess this is the best I can hope for' mindset of many of my female clients who are in very difficult, often ungodly marriages or relationships. Brant nails it: We have an epidemic of men who have been shaped and infected by distorted ideas about manhood spun from inside and outside the church. This deadly combination has produced disastrous results, impacting marriages, leadership, parenting, and humanity in general. Brant gives us hope. In his inimitable style of successfully combining profundity and humor, he calls men to understand their role as 'keeper of the garden'—provider, protector, and unselfishly present. And that is exactly what most women are looking for. This book steps into a massive gap. It's long overdue!"

Dr. Virginia Friesen, codirector of Home Improvement Ministry;
coauthor of *The Marriage App*; author of *Raising a Trailblazer*

THE
MEN
WE
NEED

THE
MEN
WE
NEED

God's Purpose for the
Manly Man, the **Avid**
Indoorsman, or **Any Man**
Willing to Show Up

BRANT HANSEN

BakerBooks

a division of Baker Publishing Group
Grand Rapids, Michigan

© 2022 by Brant Hansen

Published by Baker Books
a division of Baker Publishing Group
PO Box 6287, Grand Rapids, MI 49516-6287
www.bakerbooks.com

Printed in the United States of America

Library of Congress Cataloging-in-Publication Data
Names: Hansen, Brant, author.
Title: The men we need : God's purpose for the manly man, the avid indoorsman, or any man willing to show up / Brant Hansen.
Description: Grand Rapids, MI : Baker Books, a division of Baker Publishing Group, [2022] | Includes bibliographical references.
Identifiers: LCCN 2021035426 | ISBN 9780801094521 (paperback) | ISBN 9781540902047 (casebound) | ISBN 9781493434046 (ebook)
Subjects: LCSH: Christian men—Religious life. | Christian men—Conduct of life. | Men (Christian theology)
Classification: LCC BV4528.2 .H345 2022 | DDC 248.8/42—dc23
LC record available at https://lccn.loc.gov/2021035426

Unless otherwise indicated, Scripture quotations are from THE HOLY BIBLE, NEW INTERNATIONAL VERSION®, NIV® Copyright © 1973, 1978, 1984, 2011 by Biblica, Inc.® Used by permission. All rights reserved worldwide.

Scripture quotations labeled ESV are from The Holy Bible, English Standard Version® (ESV®), copyright © 2001 by Crossway, a publishing ministry of Good News Publishers. Used by permission. All rights reserved. ESV Text Edition: 2016

Scripture quotations labeled NKJV are from the New King James Version®. Copyright © 1982 by Thomas Nelson. Used by permission. All rights reserved.

Scripture quotations labeled NLT are from the Holy Bible, New Living Translation, copyright © 1996, 2004, 2007, 2013, 2015 by Tyndale House Foundation. Used by permission of Tyndale House Publishers, Inc., Carol Stream, Illinois 60188. All rights reserved.

The author is represented by the literary agency of The Gates Group.

To protect the privacy of those who have shared their stories with the author, some details and names have been changed.

Dedicated to all of us guys
who can't bench four hundred pounds.
And to the people
who somehow still love us.

CONTENTS

11

DECISION FIVE: Choose Today Who You Will Become Tomorrow

DECISION SIX: Take Responsibility for Your Own Spiritual Life

FOREWORD

Sherri Lynn
Brant's longtime radio producer and friend

Hunters. Fishers. Athletes. Steel mill workers.

That defines most of the men in my family. It was all I really knew. So when I met Brant Hansen, a guy who plays the flute and was the president of the Illinois Student Librarians Association, I didn't quite know what to make of him. Then one evening I went to his house for dinner. We had only been working together for maybe a week.

I was in his home less than ten minutes when I saw it. I saw what I believe to be the true definition of a man.

It wasn't him running around fixing things or watching sports. It was the way his daughter and wife looked at him.

There was love, yes. There was adoration, sure. But there was something I consider infinitely more valuable: safety. They were safe with him.

It's important to know that when I say safety, I'm speaking of more than just physical safety. You can get that from ADT. I mean they were secure in his presence. Only a deeply faithful man can provide women with that.

I grew up in a desperately unsafe household with a desperately unsafe father who was also an active, vibrant member of our church community. That has given me a better-than-average church-scoundrel radar. I felt sure Brant Hansen was *not* that, but because of my past I needed a little more proof.

Later, when we went out on the road for events, my initial impression of him was proven over and over again. When women in all of their splendor would pass us, attempting to garner some level of attention, they never had his. Never did I see him say or do anything he wouldn't have done in front of his family. There, away from his wife and daughter, he was still committed. He was still faithful. They were still safe.

In the almost decade we've worked together, I have had countless meals and events with the Hansens. The way they look at him hasn't changed. It is clear: He is still their protector.

I hounded him to write this book. For years I've watched young guys flock to him. I think it's precisely because he's not the culture's idea of "manly," yet he takes his role as protector seriously. Time after time, guys see that and want to know more. This book is the "more."

Lastly, to my sisters: *This book is for you too.*

It really is.

If you're like me and grew up with a less-than-stellar example of what manhood really is, this book will be like sweet, refreshing water to you. If you were blessed to be raised by (or are married to) a man with the attributes laid out here, you'll know to celebrate that man often.

There are so many people telling men what they shouldn't be. I truly believe Brant is the one to tell men the joy of all they could and should be—all God purposed for them when he uniquely made them men.

I'm so glad Brant has finally written this. I guess I can stop pestering him now.

A VERY IMPORTANT INTRODUCTION

Thank you for reading this. Most people skip over introductions in these sorts of books. And by "most people," I mean me. But I need you to know a couple things from the outset.

First, it's impossible to write a book about masculinity without tripping a lot of wires. And I tend to trip wires anyway without even really trying.

My friends are worried about me. "You're going to be blasted," they say.

I tell them, "Maybe. Okay, probably. But still."

I realize I'm dealing with a cultural flashpoint, but I'm not here to write a social commentary or critique. There are plenty of other options for that. And while you'll notice a lot of allusions and direct references to Scripture, this isn't a theology book per se either.

I'm here to answer a simple (but not simplistic) question: What are men supposed to actually *do*?

This book is about a big vision for manhood. We've lacked that vision, and all of us—men, women, and children—are hurting because of it.

The vision is this: *We men are at our best when we are "keepers of the garden."* This means we are protectors and defenders and cultivators. We are at our best when we champion the weak and vulnerable. We are at our best when we use whatever strength we have to safeguard the innocent and provide a place for people to thrive. This is the job Adam was given: keeper of the garden.

So I'm hoping this book is immediately practical. I hope it's full of wisdom and it adds value to your life. If you're a man reading this, I hope it inspires you to be a source of security and life for everyone around you (including those who might hate my premise that this is what men are for).

Another thing I should tell you, in full disclosure: While this book is about how to be a man, it won't be a typical How to Be a Man book because . . . I'm not capable of writing that. I don't relate to most of those books. I'm not—how to say?—the most intimidatingly "manly" of all possible men.

Let's put it this way: I don't even hunt. I play the accordion.

I'm not good at grilling. I don't even really enjoy camping. I was in Boy Scouts, but not successfully. I seriously thought the other scouts would think I was cool if I brought my new flute to the campout. (Narrator: "But they did not think it was cool, and . . .")

That's right, I play the flute too. I wanted to play sports, but since I was always one of the smallest kids in the class, our town obsession—football—was a no-go. That is, until my senior year, after I had a growth spurt and shot up to my current five feet ten. My mom then let me play high school football.

. . . Until I had to quit (and I'm not making this up) because they couldn't find a helmet big enough for my head.

I did use my oversized head successfully as captain of the Scholastic Bowl team and was all-conference. I was also the president—the *state* president—of the Illinois Student Librarians Association.

That's right. Let that soak in.

I don't know how to fix cars, though I have much respect for those who do. When I go into AutoZone, I try to play it cool, but I'm aware that they can tell I have no idea what I'm even looking at.

I'm pretty fit but not jacked. I have zero tattoos. I'm not against tats; it's just that I could never decide on one. I'm sure it would be a *Lord of the Rings* character, but there are so many. I'd hate to go with Tom Bombadil and then wish it was Elrond. I can't live with that kind of regret.

I respect hunters but don't hunt because of my neurological condition called nystagmus that makes my eyes move back and forth rapidly. In order to see, I have to move my head rapidly too. Note: Rapid, involuntary head movement is not a plus for shooting. It's not safe. Except for, you know, the animals. It's very safe for them. Deeply safe.

I say all this because I want you to know this is not going to be one of those books that's all about how, if you want to be a *real* man, you've got to get out there and take down a moose barehanded or free-solo El Capitan. I can't even free-solo stairs.

I'm an avid indoorsman. I own puppets.

But you know what? As much as, say, climbing rocks is impressive and a fine sport, the world isn't truly desperate for more people who can do that. Nothing against rock climbers. You're fantastic.

It's also true that the world's deep need isn't for more puppet-wielding accordion players. I've learned this repeatedly and emphatically.

If you do happen to be a jacked, tatted-up auto mechanic who spends his weekends spearfishing, I respect that. You're welcome here. This book is for you too.

But those things, cool as they are, aren't at the heart of what people are yearning for from us. There's something much deeper and much better. That's what this book is about.

I should also let you know that this book is written by someone who believes in God. That, of course, is not an odd thing. What may be out of the ordinary is that God is not a side character in this play. He's the central one, influencing (I hope) every page. He knows us, what we're made for, and why we're here.

Our world is hurting. People are waiting for us.

Here's hoping we can become the men we need.

KEEPER OF
THE GARDEN

The Poster

"What's the deal with the guy with the baby?"

I was asking this because a few of us were being given a tour of a women's co-op house at the University of Illinois, where I was a student, and I kept seeing the same poster seemingly in everyone's room. It was a black-and-white photo of a guy in jeans with no shirt on, sitting and holding a baby. That was it.

You've probably seen the poster. Turns out it's one of the best-selling posters of all time, with more than five million sold.

Seriously, though, the guy doesn't seem *that* muscular or remarkably exceptional. You can't even see much of his face, really. He's a model, sure, but the world isn't short of models. So what's the deal?

The female student giving us the tour answered my question. "The guy is handsome, but it's not just the guy. It's the way the baby is looking at him."

Millions of women buy a poster because of the way a baby is looking at a guy? Yes, apparently.

"The guy has his hand cradling the baby's head," the student said. "The baby is safe. We all want a guy like that."

Huh. As an eighteen-year-old guy who didn't have a girlfriend, and had never had a girlfriend, I took note of this.

I mean, I knew I couldn't look like Poster Guy, but still.

For the record, while this book isn't about making yourself attractive for women, the reaction to Poster Guy is certainly worth noting, because it may be that women instinctually want to bring out the best in us.

There's a little experiment I've conducted several times while speaking to groups of men and women or teenage girls and boys. Usually, it's while I'm talking about a subject like serving others or humility. I'll show slides of real men helping people and use actual photos from news stories: a soldier carrying an old woman out of a village, two guys helping a family into a boat during a flood, a middle-aged guy pulling a baby out of an overturned car in a canal. Some of the men are a little overweight, some balding, some covered in filth. Nobody has ripped abs. But it doesn't matter.

I'll ask a seeming non sequitur. "Oh, by the way, a question for the ladies: Do you find these men attractive?"

The response, without fail, has been immediate, vocal, and emphatic. "YEEEEEEEESSSSS!!!"

I do this because I want the males in the audience to feel the reaction. I want them to remember it, like I remembered the ubiquitous Poster Guy with Baby photo. None of these guys look like what other guys would typically think a woman freaks out about, and yet, the women freak out. Why?

Because these men are doing their thing as protectors. That's it.

Check out any survey of women being asked about the most attractive professions that men have. It's always the same: Firefighters win. Why? Because of their gigantic salary? Because of pants with awesome reflectors?

It's not pants with reflectors. I've tried this.

No, it's because they rescue people. They take responsibility for the vulnerable.

Police officers usually finish in the top five professions. So do paramedics.

I make this point to the guys in the audience: Now, you can use this information to decide, "Hey, I'm going to be a firefighting police officer so women will like me." That's one possible takeaway, sure.

But the bigger picture is that women sense who we are supposed to be. And they are attracted to us when they see us living that out. They're looking for men who make them feel secure. This is why women often consider confidence, a fit body, wealth, or a deep voice "sexy." Wise women, of course, know these are mere surface indicators and can be misleading to the extreme . . . but they're certainly hoping.

Please know this: A man who is a confident provider and protector can be less than wealthy. He can have a high-pitched voice. He can be less than fit . . . and still be very attractive to women.

Fun fact: Apparently, sometimes you don't even have to do anything to be admired for being an attractive man of action. A few nights ago, a group of loud teenage guys was out on the street in front of our house. It was after 11:00. They didn't bother me, so I sprang into inaction and stayed in bed.

> **Women sense who we are supposed to be. And they are attracted to us when they see us living that out.**

But my wife, Carolyn, was very unsettled. She couldn't sleep and watched them through the window. She went downstairs. I didn't understand what the big deal was. But I finally got out of bed.

I got dressed, went downstairs, and headed out the door to confront the guys. But as I walked outside, they all left. I didn't even do anything, and Carolyn's reaction?

I'm super hot. That's what. I didn't even do anything, and suddenly my attractiveness took a quantum jump.

Wait, I *did* do something. I showed a mere willingness to act. A *willingness* to get out of bed. A *willingness* to intervene on my wife's behalf. My wife is not a fearful person, and she didn't marry me for my awesome nunchuck skills. But women love it when we prove we're *willing* to do what needs to be done. It turns out it's not about muscle at all but about character.

In fact, if you don't prove to be a protector, if you turn out to be a man who is passive or weak of character, a woman who was once attracted to your ripped muscles will ultimately begin to resent those same ripped muscles. You will simply not have her respect, no matter how much you work out.

Women sense when we are fulfilling our purpose and when we're not. As we'll discuss, women don't respect passive men who lack ambition or drive. But it's more than that. They also grow to resent them. They know men are made for something more.

If you're married, you'll realize that your wife sees something in you—or at least saw something in you. It's the man you could be, and she's still hoping you become that. Even if she's never articulated it, she knows you're at your best when you are a source of security for those in your sphere of influence. It's alarming and annoying for her to see that role slip away. It's also profoundly disappointing.

> **What women want from us resonates entirely with the original work given the original man in the Bible's account of the garden of Eden.**

What women want from men, I believe, is a signpost pointing us to something we've all wanted: purpose. What they want from us resonates entirely with the original work given the original man in the Bible's account of the garden of Eden.

I'm hoping that by the time you've finished this book, you have a deep sense of that purpose. As I wrote in the introduction, I'm not the archetypal manly guy. Since I'm not huge, I see poorly, and I fall asleep easily, I'd be a terrible security guard. But I've found ways of serving as a protector and "keeper of the garden" with the gifts I have.

I believe you can too. With whatever you're given, you can live out this purpose, and if you do, the vulnerable people around you—and maybe those far away—will thrive and flourish because of it.

As we'll talk about a bit later, Adam was made to protect but became passive. God went looking for him. "Where are you?" he asked.

Adam left his post, and the world has been suffering ever since. It is yearning for men who show up. All kinds of men, in all walks of life, who know who they are and why they are here . . . and don't leave. Men who don't go AWOL from real life.

The world needs men to show up. You ready for this?

Masculinity Is about Taking Responsibility

"Is this the best a man can get?"

That's a voice-over in an ad Gillette debuted in 2019. The ad showed men behaving badly, preying on women and acting as bullies.

The ad continues, saying things are changing:

> There will be no going back. Because we . . . believe in the best in men. . . . To act the right way. Some already are. . . . But some is not enough. Because the boys watching today will be the men of tomorrow.[1]

The images illustrating the "act the right way" theme are of men intervening to break up fights or stopping other men from making women feel threatened. There is also a great image of a dad holding his little daughter in front of a mirror, telling her that she's strong.

The ad was a little cartoony, but I liked it. And it's apparent that the ad makers and the number of other people who also appreciated it understand that this really is what men are like when we're at our best.

As mentioned, this purpose goes back in history quite a few years. Like . . . all the way to Adam.

> Then the LORD God took the man and put him in the garden of Eden to tend and keep it. (Gen. 2:15 NKJV)

The Hebrew word translated "keep" here is *shamar*. It means "to guard," "to protect," and "to watch over."[2]

Guard. Protect. Watch over.

Think about what the garden of Eden was: A place that God and humans inhabited together. A place at peace. A place that was wildly beautiful and where things were made to thrive and to grow.

But it wasn't a finished product. There was wonderful, life-giving work to do. It needed to be shaped and enhanced. God created man and woman in his image, and that means they were made to be creative and actually *do* things that matter.

So God gave Adam the job of looking after the garden and the things within. He was to guard it, tend it, and help it flourish. He was responsible for it.

I believe looking after our own "gardens" remains our masculine purpose, and we all implicitly know it. Our culture is in chaos regarding what masculinity really is, so it's dangerous to suggest there's a distinct, wonderful thing called *masculinity*. But the Gillette commercials certainly come close.

Masculinity is about taking responsibility. We naturally respect men who take responsibility for themselves. We have even more respect for those who go beyond themselves to their families. And we have immense respect for men who take responsibility for those well outside their own homes.

We are "masculine" not to the extent that we body-build or achieve sexual conquests or fix stuff, but to the extent that we are faithful to the job of being humble, consistent, dedicated keepers of the garden. Just as Adam's failure was devastating, our failures to fill this role have been devastating.

When we do fulfill our purpose, we become a refreshing source of life wherever we are. The vulnerable will be allowed to grow and bloom. People will sense that they're safe around us. Our neighborhoods, workplaces, and homes will be safer simply because we're there. (Of course, not *everyone* will feel safe. If we are who we are made to be, those who want to attack the garden or who would threaten those within will not feel secure at all. Our mere presence will bother them.)

Keepers of the garden need not be physical brutes. What we do need is the willingness to bring whatever resources we have to fill this role in whatever contexts we find ourselves: our homes, our schools, our apartment buildings, our offices . . . anywhere we are.

The original garden was a place where God was fully in charge as King and his justice and peace were present, to everyone's benefit. We were supposed to rule with him and to expand his rule, but we misused our freedom. He has promised he will one day restore it all, and the biblical glimpses we get of the kingdom in its fullness are breathtaking. Glimpses like the lame leaping like deer, every tear being wiped from our eyes, and the deaf getting to hear for the first time.

We get to be part of expanding that kingdom here and now in the places we find ourselves. Not as a power move, but quite the opposite: through humility. You are made to do this, whether you're a student, an accountant, a motorcycle mechanic, or a drive-through worker at Burger King.

Maybe you're a nerd like me, or maybe you play left tackle for the Seahawks. Doesn't matter.

Maybe you're outwardly healthy; maybe you're battling an obvious disability. Doesn't matter.

Wealthy or poor? Makes no difference.

We're all called to be keepers and protectors in our spheres of influence, whatever and wherever they are.

The way Jesus explains the kingdom of God (and he talks about it more than anything else in the Gospels), it works very differently from the rest of the world. The weak are made strong. The last are first. The humble are exalted. The proud are brought low. The widow, the alien, and the orphan are valued highly. The unfairly treated are defended. The seemingly insignificant go to the head of the class. The lost are found. And the broken are healed.

> **You are made to do this, whether you're a student, an accountant, a motorcycle mechanic, or a drive-through worker at Burger King.**

Imagine men like you and me taking whatever strength we are given to defend and expand that kingdom rather than our own temporary, throwaway, little ones that will never last.

Imagine if we approached life like this: "Adam didn't do the job. But with whatever I have, I'm going to do it. I have a mission, and I accept it."

In the Bible, God says he raises the poor from the dust. He doesn't forget them. He defends the afflicted. He saves the children of the needy. He defends the weak. He favors the humble. (See 1 Sam. 2:8; Pss. 9:18; 72:4; 82:3; Prov. 3:34.)

If I'm going to be more like him, guess what I'm going to do? I'm going to raise the poor from the dust. I won't forget them. I will defend the afflicted. I will save the children of the needy. I will defend the weak. I will favor the humble.

Jesus told us to seek his kingdom first. When we take our cues from him, it's not just good news for us. It's good news for everyone around us.

We Need You Out Here, Man

So what exactly does Adam do when the garden is threatened? We don't know for certain, but it sure looks like he does the following:

1. Absolutely nothing.

Maybe you know the story. After God gives Adam his assignment to protect and tend the garden, he tells Adam not to eat from the Tree of the Knowledge of Good and Evil.

God then creates Eve, a "suitable helper" for Adam. The word for "helper," *ezer*, shouldn't be read as "assistant" or "underling." God himself is described as *ezer* in Psalms. He is our helper because he has the ability to aid us in our need. He rescues us because we need rescuing. An ezer is distinctly "other" from us and is a lifesaver. An ezer is not our mere sidekick.

Women were to be corulers with men from the very start. In Genesis 1, God creates mankind in his own image, "male and female," and then he blesses them and tells them to be fruitful, increase in number, and rule over the earth. Again, that's not just for the male. Male and female are made to rule, together.

Later, Eve has a conversation in the garden with an enemy of God. The enemy claims she's missing out by accepting the limits God had given to Adam.

She falls for the lie. She eats the fruit. And all the while, Adam doesn't do anything.

Now, where do you think Adam was when all this was happening? When I heard this story as a kid, I'd always pictured Adam far away, doing some hard work or something while Eve was dealing with the snaky enemy. But notice where Adam actually is:

> When the woman saw that the fruit of the tree was good for food and pleasing to the eye, and also desirable for gaining wisdom, she took some and ate it. She also gave some to her husband, *who was with her*, and he ate it. Then the eyes of both of them were opened, and they realized they were naked; so they sewed fig leaves together and made coverings for themselves. (Gen. 3:6–7, italics mine)

The text makes it seem like Adam was there the whole time. So he let her converse with an enemy of God, and he didn't intervene to protect her or the garden.

Adam, remarkably, did nothing, and I say "remarkably" because we're still remarking on it thousands of years later. That's how impactful our refusals to act can be.

Adam was so passive he didn't even grab any fruit for himself. It says Eve passed it to him. Maybe he was lying down!

This is a fundamental betrayal of who he is supposed to be. He's supposed to guard the garden and all the beautiful things in it. He's supposed to rule and reign with God. Instead, he just stands there. Or maybe he's lying in a hammock while the world

> Adam was so passive he didn't even grab any fruit for himself. It says Eve passed it to him. Maybe he was lying down?

takes a blow we still haven't recovered from. It's something we're still ashamed of. In fact, it introduced shame itself into the world.

Next, get this:

> The man and his wife heard the sound of the LORD God as he was walking in the garden in the cool of the day, and they hid from the LORD God among the trees of the garden. But the LORD God called to the man, "Where are you?"
>
> He answered, "I heard you in the garden, and I was afraid because I was naked; so I hid." (vv. 8–10)

So the woman eats the fruit first, and she has been blamed for that for millennia. But notice God doesn't call *her* out. No. He wants to know where the man is. The security guard.

Where are you, Adam?

Now, to be sure, they're both in trouble. The fact that God comes looking for Adam doesn't mean he's more significant than Eve. But where's the keeper of the garden? Where's the one God specifically charged with being the protector?

Where's the one he made to take responsibility?

Given our current human condition, it may be that God is still asking.

This brings us to a possibly dangerous question to bat around with friends.

Let's say "Jake" is a relatively physically healthy nineteen-year-old. He lives at his parents' house and stays inside almost all day, every day. He spends his time playing video games and watching porn. His parents provide meals and snacks. He's content. He'd say he's happy with his life.

Is this okay? I mean, is there anything really "wrong" with this?

He's happy, right? He's not bothering anyone else. He's harming no one else.

Is there actually a problem?

For some, the answer will be obvious: No. There really isn't a problem at all, because as long as he's not hurting anyone else and he's happy, what does it matter? We should all be free to construct our own realities, and that's what it means to be human.

But this reasoning doesn't quite work. It presumes that freedom to do whatever we want is what we should value most. How do we know that?

And it also ignores this: Jake *is* actually harming himself and others, by not being who he was created to be. The world needs Jake. There are real humans outside his window who will suffer because he isn't who we need him to be. There are real humans outside *your* window who will suffer because you aren't who we need you to be.

> **There are real humans outside *your* window who will suffer because you aren't who we need you to be.**

There are perhaps thousands of people whose lives will be worse—possibly for decades—because Jake is a no-show.

He also may currently be "happy," but who decreed that mere happiness is the end goal? After all, it can and will be fleeting. Maybe we should pursue something bigger and richer and longer lasting than that.

Now, Jake may not look like the idealized hero, but he could decide to be one. Like all of us, he's been given a measure of strength and intelligence and creativity. He's been given resources to fill a certain role. We'll talk more about those things, but these are worth thinking about now:

> While Jake immerses himself in fake accomplishments, there are real things that need to be done.
>
> While he entertains himself with images of women, there are real women yearning for actual grown-up men.

While his games and entertainment may center on fake story-
lines of fighting injustice, there are real people who need
protection.

Everything Jake has is given to him for a reason, including his
freedom. It really is up to him whether he chooses life through the
real or death through the fake.

He's like all of us. This is where we are right now. This Jake,
like the original Adam, was created to be a keeper of the garden, a
protector and defender. He was created to make order from chaos.
He was created to help the things and people around him thrive
and grow in beauty and strength.

But he's AWOL. He's taking the passive route.

It's simply not enough for someone to say about their life,
"I didn't bother anybody." (Interestingly, where older religious
traditions—attributed to Buddha and Confucius, for example—
held the Golden Rule to be, essentially, "Don't do to others what
you don't want done to you," Jesus goes well beyond that: "In
everything, *do* to others what you would have them do to you"
[Matt. 7:12, italics mine].)

Do. Actively meet needs. Actively show up. Actively engage.

Man was created to take responsibility. So if a guy's life is all
about entertainment options, using women for sexual pleasure,
smoking some weed, and modifying his car, he's not yet a man.
He's stuck in boydom. God loves him dearly, yes, and I'm rooting
for him. But he's not the man the world needs him to be. Not yet.
Wow, do we need him to grow up.

Some boys start becoming men early. If you're a dad or mom
reading this and you have, say, an eight-year-old boy, you can ignite
his imagination by helping him understand his role as a defender
and keeper of the garden. He won't resist this. Boys tend to love
challenges and knowing their roles, especially when they happen
to fit a deep yearning.

If your son picks on his little sister (like mine did), you can remind him why this is a very bad thing. He's betraying the role he was given. He's to be her protector, not a threat to her. My son understood this very clearly, and he took it to heart. I'm proud of the man he has become. (Dad-brag alert: At this writing, he's currently an intelligence officer in the military, planning to become a surgeon at CURE Hospitals to serve children with disabilities in developing nations.)

Young kids can understand this role. Certainly nineteen-year-olds can understand it.

Jake, we need you out here.

A Quick Word about Toxic Passivity

Let's review a bit.

When the garden was faced with a threat, Adam did nothing.

When Eve was under spiritual attack, Adam did nothing.

When Eve offered him fruit, Adam took the path of least resistance.

When God came into the garden to speak to him, Adam hid.

When God confronted him with what he did, Adam made up excuses and blamed Eve.

At no point in this story is Adam doing his job. He is passive.

He was not created to be passive. Humans were not created to evade responsibility, hide from God, or make up excuses and deflect the blame.

A passive man becomes useless to those around him. What's more—and this may seem counterintuitive—a passive man is a *threat* to the woman in his life.

A man's passivity makes a woman feel less secure, because she will intuit that he may not be up to the job of defending her or their home. He may not be up to the job of providing for her and their children. He may even become a drag on her own ambitions. She may feel like she's somewhat on her own, even if they're married, and needs to frenetically cover all of life's bases because he may not do it.

It's very unsettling, and you know what? It's also weirdly common.

My friends Paul and Virginia Friesen are both PhDs and family counselors. They say passive men are a far more common problem in their practice than men who are overbearing, physically intimidating, or the other usual things we consider examples of toxic masculinity.

"It can seem benign," Paul told me. "A husband finds it's easier to check out mentally and emotionally and concentrate on work, for instance. He just says, 'Yes, dear' or something like that to keep the peace, but it winds up being the downfall of the home."

> **A man's passivity makes a woman feel less secure, because she will intuit that he may not be up to the job of defending her or their home.**

We don't want to be like this. Nobody admires a passive man. People don't buy movie tickets to watch men without a mission. There is no Whatever-Man hero in the Marvel universe.

Passive-Man is a disappointment at best and a threat at worst. The good news is, you can make a decision right now to be different.

Don't be Passive-Man. Or his underperforming fellow superhero, Blaming-Guy. No one respects him either.

The Ancient Art of Blaming Other People

When Adam fails to do his job, he deals with it like most of us tend to deal with things: He finds somebody else to blame.

Since there's only one other person around, I guess the choice is easy. It's *that woman.*

> The LORD God called to the man, "Where are you?"
>
> He answered, "I heard you in the garden, and I was afraid because I was naked; so I hid."
>
> And he said, "Who told you that you were naked? Have you eaten from the tree that I commanded you not to eat from?"
>
> The man said, "*The woman you put here with me*—she gave me some fruit from the tree, and I ate it." (Gen. 3:9–12, italics mine)

Let's think about this. Here's what we know:

Genesis was written thousands of years ago.

It tells the story of the first man.

The first time the first man does something wrong, he blames someone else.

Sounds . . . believable. This is how we roll.

It's not just men, of course, who are prone to blaming others. It's everybody. But what Adam does is especially jarring when we remember his very first reaction to the woman: He's utterly smitten. He waxes poetic. His first words—the first words of the first man in the Bible!—are rhapsodic about the wonder of this magnificent creature, this "woman"!

And then his next words in Scripture are blaming that magnificent creature.

Adam pivots from describing her this way:

> This is now bone of my bones
>   and flesh of my flesh;
> she shall be called "woman,"
>   for she was taken out of man. (Gen. 2:23)

To describing her this way:

The woman you put here with me. (Gen. 3:12)

That's quite a transition. "Oh, the rapture! She is my flesh! We are but one! United forever and ev— Wait, what? THAT WOMAN DID IT."

Notice that the first man pulls off an impressive Double Blame Move, wherein he's actually blaming God too for putting "the woman" there in the first place. He does this in just a few words. As a veteran blame shifter myself (I seriously once blamed the crowd for my loss during a spelling bee), I almost admire the craftsmanship of the Double Blame Move.

We are geniuses at blaming other people. (I wrote a whole book about this—*The Truth about Us*.) Our ability to do this is a superpower, and we all have it. It's stunning that refusing to take responsibility is so human, so obvious, and so widespread that the writer of Genesis tells us the very first man does it.

Adam's failure to protect the garden is on him. But he doesn't want to believe it. Who's he trying to fool, exactly? God? No, he's fooling himself.

And that's just it. The world doesn't need more excuses, but we keep manufacturing them by the score, in ways both subtle and obvious.

Allow me an example, in the form of a provocative question for people who are Jesus followers:

Q: A very attractive woman wears a dress that is revealing. A man nearby decides to fantasize about having sex with her. Who's at fault for his decision?

(A) She is.

(B) He is.

(C) Mostly him, but she's culpable too because she shouldn't be wearing stuff like that.

(D) Neither, because there's nothing wrong with the man's fantasy, and Jesus never really emphasized this sort of thing or talked about it. We should focus on real issues.

I will give you the correct answer.

It's B. He's at fault. Completely.

A, C, and D are all excuses.

D uses a false claim to provide an excuse—that Jesus didn't talk about lust or regard it as a "real issue." He certainly did, and the entire Bible is full of both warnings about lust and examples of the devastating effects of it.

The woman is not at fault. It's not even 90/10. She's not at fault at all.

"But," you might say, "she should really dress more appropriately. It's wrong to dress that way."

But that wasn't the question, was it? The question was about who is ultimately responsible for the *man's* behavior, and the answer is . . . the *man.*

You and I are 100 percent responsible for whether we decide to fantasize about someone. That's our call. Now, noticing a woman is not an act of will. Noticing that she's extremely attractive is not an act of will either. But a refusal to restrain our imagination and instead engage it is an act of will. We can look away, and we can move our minds to other distractions, if we so choose.

This is on us. Is it difficult, if you're in the habit of getting a sexual "buzz" from looking at women? Absolutely. But it's not at all impossible. Again, we're not talking about merely noticing or even appreciating a woman's attractiveness. We're talking about our decisions from there.

Don't do the Double Blame Move. Don't do the "It's that woman you gave me" thing. Own it.

None of this is a guilt trip. It's actually empowering. Would you rather be a helpless victim, at the mercy of whoever walks by or appears on a billboard? We're not powerless. We don't have to lust. We can actually take our thoughts captive.

I'm just using the question above as an example. It's remarkable how good we are at shifting an argument or even fashioning a whole new worldview in order to dodge blame. We're sophisticated about it.

To properly keep and protect our garden—the people and things around us that need us to grow up—we can't be blame shifters. Since masculinity is about the taking of responsibility, it means squarely owning up to our own failures and the things we need to do.

You should know that people will find you *very* refreshing if you're not a blame shifter. It's a rare, beautiful, and strong thing.

You have the responsibility of guarding your heart. You have the say in whether you will allow God to shape who you are becoming. No one else will do this for you.

Remember Judas? He was in Jesus' inner circle. He had the best teacher of all time right there with him. He had the best counselor ever, the best leader, the best spiritual shepherd. He saw miracles firsthand. But he wasn't transformed.

That's on him.

Jesus tells a story about three servants who were given money to invest while the master was away, and when the master came back, two of them had multiplied his money. The other didn't. Instead, he offered excuses. It's clear from the story that all of us have a responsibility for how we conduct our lives.

You have the say in whether you will allow God to shape who you are becoming. No one else will do this for you.

Again, this is not bad news. It's wonderful. It means that if you intend to be the man God created you to be and the man we need you to be, you have the means to do so. That goal is not out of reach. It's not up to others.

I love this quote from habit expert James Clear:

> A profitable business is never a choice, it is a series of choices.
> A fit body is never a choice, it is a series of choices.
> A strong relationship is never a choice, it is a series of choices.[1]

You make choices. They matter. They are yours. Yes, some of your choices will be selfish, immature, and foolish. But own them. Learn from them. Continue to bring your attention back to God (we'll talk about this later) and watch how he changes you over time to become the sort of person who more naturally chooses the right things, the wise things.

Those are the things that give life to you and everyone else in your garden.

The Scariest Thing

We humans actually like being scared—under certain controlled conditions. Some people go to haunted houses or watch horror movies. Some people like the feeling of cheating death by riding roller coasters, skydiving, or bungee jumping off a bridge. Some people are Detroit Lions fans.

But if you want to do something truly terrifying, spend time pondering this possibility: You might never become the man you were intended to become.

Think about the horror of looking back on your life and realizing it was all about you. Whatever you wanted, when you wanted it: gaming, doing drugs, having porn fantasies, using women, trying to collect experiences, and buying some stuff. That's it. Your days just rolled by.

You committed to no one but yourself. You chose to insulate yourself from anything that would call you out to be a man. None of the things you sought forced you to go beyond yourself. Whenever you were called to sacrifice and there wasn't anything in it for you, you said no. You were loyal to no one, ultimately, but you.

You never became who we needed you to be.

Picture that, and then picture the inevitable result: You're now utterly alone. Because that's where living to fulfill your own desires, however disordered, eventually leads.

Real commitments to real people and real causes make you grow up. If you commit to a real woman, you won't be able to just conjure up any woman in your mind and then, when the sexual thrill is over, move on to something else that gives you stimulation. Nope. A real-life woman will test you in a thousand wonderful ways.

Fantasies never tell you to stop playing games and go to bed. Real women do. Fantasies never ask you tough questions about why you bought that thing you bought when you're on a tight budget. Real women do. Fantasies don't get sick, wake you up at 2:00 a.m., and ask you to get up, get dressed, and run to CVS. Real women do.

Fantasies don't argue with you. They don't challenge your claims about yourself. They don't make you angry. They don't require you to develop mercy and grace under pressure. They don't call you out to be a strong protector, a servant and guard of the vulnerable around you. They don't call you out to be a hero.

> **Fantasies never tell you to stop playing games and go to bed. Real women do. Fantasies never ask you tough questions about why you bought that thing you bought when you're on a tight budget. Real women do.**

But real women do. They will call you out to become a keeper of the garden.

It's not only a wife who can help you become the man we need you to be. Working with a variety of people, exercising, making friends, and maintaining relationships with family members are all things that can push you to be who you should be. But marriage is an obvious example of making a commitment to serve a real human, no matter what, and the growth that comes from that. Marriage is hard, and the first indicator of that truth is that it usually starts with a vow to never quit made in front of a large group of people.

Lots of hard things start with a vow, actually. Lots of very good, very hard things. My wife and I got to watch our son, Justice, take a vow. He vowed that he would defend the Constitution of the United States against all enemies, "bear true faith and allegiance" to the Constitution, and faithfully discharge the duties of an Air Force officer.

He excelled, but it was not easy. He knew it wouldn't be. He anticipated that he would be asked every day—every hour, possibly—to do things he didn't feel like doing in the moment. He grew as a man.

This growth starts with loyalty, with a commitment. "No matter what, I am going to do this." That's a vow.

Marriage and the military will call you to grow up. So will other commitments to causes and people and missions bigger than you.

In our affluent Western culture, growing up for many of us is weirdly optional. Historically, men have had no choice but to grow up. They had to work to eat. They had to defend themselves, their families, and their communities. But most of us here and now can choose the life of an entertainment consumer, just moving from one experience to the next.

And then we're shocked at the prevailing sense of meaninglessness. (A recent headline in a UK paper about sixteen-to-twenty-nine-year-olds reads, "Nine in Ten Young Brits Believe Their Life Lacks Purpose, according to Shocking New Study."[1])

This sounds harsh to our modern ears, but Jesus taught it: We can make ourselves completely useless. We're supposed to be salt, but salt can lose its saltiness. And then what good is it? It's worthless (Matt. 5:13). Anyone who doesn't remain in him, he says, is like a useless branch that withers and then gets thrown into a pile and burned. It has lost its value, its purpose (John 15:6).

> **This sounds harsh to our modern ears, but Jesus taught it: We can make ourselves completely useless.**

Earlier, we mentioned the three men in Jesus' story who were entrusted with their boss's money while the boss was away. When he came back, he learned that two of them had worked to invest the money and had made a profit. The third just buried what he had been given. He did nothing with it.

The boss was not pleased with that guy. At least, I sense some displeasure—reading between the lines here—and perhaps you'll pick up on that subtle vibe when he says, "Throw that worthless servant outside, into the darkness, where there will be weeping and gnashing of teeth" (Matt. 25:30).

He seems upset.

Again, if you want to be freaked out by something, don't bother with the haunted house tour. Be freaked out by the very real possibility that you never become the man you could have been, that we needed you to be, because it was all about you.

But don't stay freaked out about it. It's up to you. You can change your course. It's simply a matter of intending to do what you need to do to fulfill your purpose.

It really does have to be intentional. Most good things don't just happen. If you want to become a doctor, for instance, you can't do it by just wondering, *Will I ever become a doctor?* There are decisions to be made, steps to be taken.

None of us are experts in this, but in the pages ahead, I'll talk about what I've learned so far. Hopefully it's wisdom that will be incredibly practical for you. Hopefully it'll add value not just to your life but to the lives of those around you: family, friends, coworkers, and even your enemies.

Let's do this.

THE SIX DECISIONS THAT WILL SET YOU APART

Decision One

Forsake the Fake
and Relish the Real

The Fake Life
and Where It Leads

Ever get ripped off?

This is going to sound especially dumb—I'm being vulnerable here—but we got ripped off during the COVID-19 quarantine. Everybody was hogging all the toilet paper around town, so I outflanked them (I apologize for that pun. But I'm leaving it here, so am I *really* sorry?) and ordered twelve rolls on Amazon.

When they arrived, there were twelve rolls, all right. Twelve remarkably tiny rolls. For elves. For like forty bucks. All twelve rolls could fit in a single shoebox. I laughed until I realized, "Okay, but seriously. We still need some toilet paper."

Yes, I fell for the ol' Tiny Toilet Paper Swindle, which brings to mind an important Chinese book, *The Book of Swindles*. I'm not really an expert on this book. I just found out about it while googling ten minutes ago. But apparently it lists twenty-four different kinds of swindles, with categories like "Misrepresentation" and "False Relations" and, awkwardly, a category just called "Women." It was written in the 1600s, and commenters say it's quite relevant for today. This is because, while technology has developed over the centuries, humans haven't changed that much. We're always falling for things. We're convinced we're getting one thing and wind up with another.

Adam and Eve come back to mind. And then there's this from about 2,700 years ago:

> Food gained by fraud tastes sweet,
>> but one ends up with a mouth full of gravel. (Prov. 20:17)

There are two reasons this proverb is beautiful. First, because you absolutely need to name your next hip-hop-tinged, neo-punk band "Mouth of Gravel." But you already knew this.

And secondly, it's just so true. There's this sweet taste—at first. Then there's a dark turn, and we're left with bitterness and pain. That's how sin works. Always promising, initially exciting, this rush of freedom . . . and then the punch in the gut.

Of course, when Adam and Eve got swindled, they were promised something, and it seemed to them like a better plan than what God was offering. So they went for it.

Think about how we commonly destroy our lives based on some version of that swindle. Few people have this plan: "I'm going to get addicted to this [substance or activity], and I'm going to destroy my life and family with it."

No, it always starts with excitement, with a burst of what truly feels life-giving, and then . . . you know, mouth full of gravel.

And you're by yourself.

The enemy—a swindler from the beginning—has a plan: Isolate us. He won't advertise it that way. Isolation never seems to be the goal, but it's always the end result.

And then there's Jesus, who "is before all things, and in him all things hold together," Paul writes in Colossians 1:17. God's plan is for things to come together, under his authority. Real life leads us toward each other, not away.

Years ago, I read an account of a woman who had been a girl-friend to all sorts of top athletes in the NBA and NFL. Looking back on her years of sleeping with stars, she told a reporter something I couldn't forget: "I really thought one of them would love me."

Sounds familiar. At the deepest level, that's all of us. We earnestly thought *this* would happen, but *that* happened instead. We're constantly subject to the swindle, and it's always heartbreaking. It's always a sucker punch. The things that seem to give us more life in the moment are shortcuts and fakes that leave us with less life. They seem like a way to a real payoff, what we're really looking for. But they're not going to pay off. They're going to rob us.

Yuri Tolochko is a bodybuilder who looks like an action hero. He's massively muscular with a full, manly beard. He also "married" a sex doll. Apparently there are conflicts in his relationship with the lifeless toy, like when he "forbade her from Instagram." He said, "Maybe I'm being too selfish. But that's the beauty of Margo, that I can do this to her and she won't mind."[1]

Exactly. This "woman" isn't a woman, and now you're not the man we needed you to be.

At the time of this writing, the sale of sex dolls and robots is booming. *Forbes* magazine reported a spike of 51 percent in just one recent two-month period. "We have lots of products in stock but we can't work fast enough to keep up with demand," one company founder said.[2]

One robot-selling company says the driver behind the sales isn't just sexual pleasure. It's *connection*. "We have combined the best features of the female mind and body. . . . This means not only can you enjoy their sexuality, but you can also connect with her on a human intimate level. She will emanate comfort and safety from her warm body allowing the intimacy to grow over time." Your robot will tell you the weather, ask about your day, and help you "have the mental stimulation you have always craved."[3]

Looks real. Acts real, even empathetic. Makes you feel like you have an "intimate" relationship that the manufacturers know you're really yearning for. Provides you with a dopamine hit.

And after it's over, after you've tricked your own brain and body parts, it's just you and yourself and some plastic. That's it.

Just you. Again. Alone.

It's another con job designed to stop you from fulfilling your role. It has the veneer of womanhood, of companionship, but instead of calling you out to be a man, it makes you less of one. You needn't take responsibility.

"The best features of the female mind . . ." That's another lie within the lie. The real female mind adds to us, challenges us, complements us, confounds us, confronts us, and makes us grow up.

Funny how handing ourselves over to our desires always ultimately leaves us in the same place. God created us for relationship, but we get swindled into isolation.

> **The real female mind adds to us, challenges us, complements us, confounds us, confronts us, and makes us grow up.**

And that's where sin ultimately leads. We think of sin as rebellion against God, but it rarely looks like abject rebellion. Instead, it's a sly replacement of a good thing with something quietly deadly, something ultimately hollow. It promises life but delivers a death blow. Pornography and sex with plastic are the obvious examples of taking something great, something beautifully life-giving and relational, and then, abraca-presto, turning it into soul-killing loneliness.

My sin isn't sin because it's on a random list of activities that God just doesn't happen to like. *My sin is sin because it stops me from being who I'm supposed to be and what I could have been.* It's a shortcut that leads away from the kingdom of God, where I can flourish, to a different kingdom—the kingdom of me.

There's another word for the kingdom of Brant Hansen, under the absolute authority of Brant Hansen, led by the unfettered desires of Brant Hansen.

It's called hell.

"That's Not a Girl.
That's a Piece of Paper."

Honestly, I feel sorry for us. It's not supposed to be this way.

I think you and I are up against circumstances the likes of which men of previous generations haven't faced. There's been wisdom literature for centuries (like Proverbs 5) warning men against destroying their lives by giving in to disordered sexual desires. But there has never before been a time like this, a time when we can so easily get drawn into something both exceptionally dangerous and nearly omnipresent: "supernormal stimuli." And it's worth talking about, because it can destroy everything in your life.

Some famous research on supernormal stimuli was conducted by Nikolaas Tinbergen, who should be saluted for being (1) a Nobel Prize winner and (2) the person with the most Dutch-sounding name of all time. He seriously sounds like a guy who, every Christmas, climbs down your windmill and gives you ice skates.

Anyway, Tinbergen wanted to find out if birds would prefer to sit on fake eggs if the eggs had more defined markings, had more color, or were bigger. And they did. The exaggerated eggs were hard to resist.

He also wanted to find out if a particular territorial fish—the male stickleback—would more aggressively attack a rival fish if the rival's underside was more red than usual. He made some fake wooden stickleback fish and painted their undersides an exaggerated bright red. The real fish attacked like crazy. The redder the fish, the more the reaction.

Tinbergen also wondered about sexual attraction and butterflies. He constructed a fake female butterfly out of cardboard. The model was rudimentary and unrealistic, but he gave it the exaggerated markings of female butterflies, using more vivid colors. Would the males be more attracted to the fake, exaggerated female?

You bet they were. And how. They tried to mate with the fake butterfly. They were entranced.

Beautiful, real females waited nearby . . . but they couldn't compete. They had no chance. They were now ignored.

When it came to stimulation, the real simply couldn't compete with the exaggerated fake.

Sound familiar?

We humans have the same problem. We'll go for the exaggerated fake, and we lose our appetite for the real. Although this desire is distorted, it's not the deepest tragedy here.

The deepest tragedy is that giving in to our desire for the fake distorts *us*. Psychologically. Sexually. Even physically.

We become less real. Less human.

> **When it came to stimulation, the real simply couldn't compete with the exaggerated fake.**

"Supernormal stimuli are a driving force in many of today's problems, including obesity, addiction to television and video games, and war," writes Deirdre Barrett, author of *Supernormal Stimuli*. "People sit alone in front of a plastic box streaming *Friends* instead of going out with their real buddies. They tend FarmVille crops while shirking their real duties. Men have sex with two-dimensional screen images when a willing partner may be in the next room."[1]

Few people would say this is really how they want to live. But this is where we are. Real life, with its real risks and slower rhythms, struggles to compete with the short-term payoff we can get from pixels.

None of us really want the kind of life that's spent relating to images instead of our actual wives. I love this bit from a Kurt Vonnegut novel, when the character Fred hands Harry a photo of a woman in a bikini.

> He nudged Harry, man-to-man.
> "Like that, Harry?" he asked.
> "Like what?"
> "The girl there."
> "That's not a girl. That's a piece of paper."[2]

It's the ol' swindle again, and Harry knows it. That's not a woman at all. It's ink.

Or it's an arrangement of pixels on a screen. It's a binary code. It's nothing, really.

Nothing at all.

Make no mistake, when we throw ourselves into nothingness, a sense of meaninglessness is not far behind. And reducing our lives to meaninglessness is the goal of our spiritual enemy. God loads meaning into the world, and the enemy wants to deconstruct it. That's all he can do—tear down or offer a mockery of the real thing.

As Tinbergen demonstrated, this isn't just about sex. We can replace the good with the destructive and meaningless in any number of arenas.

Junk food is a great example. It takes the taste of natural food and exaggerates it. It makes it more appealing. And there are new junk foods arriving by the minute with still more stimulation. Our tastes get distorted. They begin to change, and the food that every cell in our body needs us to eat gets ignored . . . while we reach for Ding Dongs and Doritos. And as always, we're ultimately left unsatisfied.

We're addicted to the dopamine hit we can get from supernormal stimuli, but here's the reason it's an unending treadmill: The dopamine never gives us what we're really looking for.

Susan Weinschenk is a psychologist who wrote that dopamine doesn't actually bring us pleasure. It merely makes us keep looking for more. "The latest research shows that dopamine causes seeking behavior. Dopamine causes us to want, desire, seek out, and search," she wrote. It "doesn't have satiety built in. . . . This constant stimulation of the dopamine system can be exhausting. We are getting caught in an endless dopamine loop," she continues, noting that it's actually the opioid system that gives us the "I like this" feedback. But the opioid system is weaker than the dopamine loop. So, she says, "We seek more than we are satisfied."[3]

This explains so much. Think about it. If you are using porn, are you doing it because you have such a strong sex drive? I remember hearing from many of my friends that they couldn't resist because their sex drive was just so strong. But that surely means you shouldn't require further visual stimulation, right? Why are you feeding your mind new images? Why throw gas on the fire when it's already raging?

Because it's not about the lust at all. It's about the search. We're looking for something, and it's perhaps not what we think. "The young man who rings the bell at the brothel is unconsciously looking for God," Scottish writer Bruce Marshall famously said.[4]

It's not about the lust at all. It's about the search.

It may not seem like it, but there is a longing in us far more powerful than lust. Yet lust is what's on offer from our culture, and it always promises something it never delivers. "Lust," Frederick Buechner wrote, "is the craving for salt of a man who is dying of thirst."[5]

Like I said, I feel sorry for us. It's not supposed to be this diffi-cult. It hasn't always been this way. Most men throughout history haven't had supernormal stimuli available at any time and any place. We're living in a remarkably difficult time. If you struggle with this, you're in the vast majority.

But here we are, and as easily as we can become waylaid by this struggle, the world desperately needs men with a larger vision for themselves. It needs men who resist distortion, who engage reality at all times, and who are fully real themselves.

Here's Some Good News about Pornography. No, Really.

So here's a chapter specifically about pornography, and I promise it's not a guilt trip. We already know we're all messed up and our culture is messed up. But it's remarkable to see *how* evil works in our lives and exactly *how* the fake can destroy the real.

What the brain mistakenly thinks is sex is actually killing real sex. And what the brain thinks is connection is killing real connection. Pornography is actually ruining sex for millions, causing even young men to have trouble being aroused by actual, real-life women. The Italian Society for Andrology and Sexual Medicine put it bluntly: "Internet porn is killing young men's sexual performance."[1] They simply can't relate to real women anymore, even if they want to. Why? Porn exposure has literally made their brains different. (We'll talk more about that shortly.)

According to urologist Dr. Carlo Foresta, the number of high school teenagers reporting low sexual desire increased 600 percent between 2004 and 2013. There was a pronounced difference between frequent porn users and infrequent ones.[2]

Why? What on earth happened between 2004 and 2013? Wild guess: smartphones.

"It starts with lower reactions to porn sites," Dr. Foresta said. "Then, there is a drop in libido, and in the end, it becomes impossible to get an erection."[3]

Porn use means sexual problems. It's a fact, not a moral argument (though there are plenty of moral arguments to advance here). And that's fascinating, because we again see how the fake is not benign. The lie serves to destroy the real and the true and the beautiful.

Psychologist Philip Zimbardo writes extensively about "arousal addiction." The reward circuitry in our brains is made for real life, the real world we live in, and real situations humans find themselves in. It's not made for the constant flow of dopamine hits from pornography use.

What's more, he says, there are physical changes that porn use triggers in the brain. That's dangerous for all of us, but *particularly* for young men, whose brains are still developing.[4]

The toll isn't strictly about sexual performance. Gary Wilson, in his TED Talk called "The Great Porn Experiment," talks about the mental health consequences of porn use:

> Arousal addiction symptoms are easily mistaken for such things as ADHD, social anxiety, depression, concentration problems, performance anxiety, OCD, and a host of others. Now, healthcare providers often assume that these conditions are primary, perhaps the cause of addiction, but never really the result of an addiction. As a consequence, they often medicate these guys without really inquiring about whether they have an internet addiction. So guys never realize they can overcome these symptoms simply by changing their behavior.[5]

Think about that. Depression, ADHD, concentration problems . . . all possibly (not always, of course, but perhaps often) rooted in addiction to arousal.

Porn keeps us from being who we're supposed to be. But you knew that. It works like any other addiction: It numbs our ability to derive pleasure from simple day-to-day life. To get our dopamine hit, we've got to turn back to the only thing that will provide it.

But there's good news. Thankfully, a lot of people are finding that dramatic healing can happen pretty fast. Wilson quotes one man's experience giving up pornography:

> I've been to psychologists and psychiatrists for the last eight years. Have been diagnosed with depression, severe social anxiety, severe memory impairment, and a few others. Have tried Effexor, Ritalin, Xanax, Paxil. Dropped out of two different colleges, been fired twice, used pot to calm my social anxiety. I've been approached by quite a few women, I guess due to my looks and status, but they quickly flew away due to my incredible weirdness.
>
> I've been a hard-core porn addict since age fourteen. For the last two years, I've been experimenting and finally realized that porn was an issue. I stopped it completely two months ago. It's been very difficult, but so far, incredibly worth it. I've since quit my remaining medication. My anxiety is nonexistent. My memory and focus are sharper than they've ever been. . . . I seriously think I had a rebirth, a second chance at life.[6]

There's an online community at Reddit strictly about giving up porn, and more than 700,000 people belong to it. It's refreshing to read. The stories of what happens when guys get their minds away from porn are encouraging. One seventeen-year-old writes:

> I went from an introvert to an extrovert: not overnight, of course, but it was a slow process of getting more and more confidence to go out and not worry about talking to random strangers, and making new friends. . . . This has made life much, much easier for me.[7]

From others on the Reddit forum:

I found a girl who actually made me a man. She realised me, how I was irresponsible towards my family. I started spending time with my family and being that son again.[8]

[On the benefits of going 284 days without porn.] I feel happier, more relaxed, less like I need a hit of dopamine. . . . I feel more in control of my life now.[9]

I had serious anger issues [when using porn]. . . . The two are DEFINITELY related. Watching porn . . . changes our brain's chemical makeup so much that irritation/anger becomes a dominant emotion.[10]

[After going ninety days without porn.] I can feel more emotions, I'm more confident . . . I'm more motivated for school.[11]

None of this may be surprising to you. You may already know, or at least suspect, that porn is actually making your life worse in many ways. You may already know how it distorts and destroys. But you may have also found that simply knowing isn't enough. We need more.

We need a bigger vision for our lives.

We have to want something *more* than we want the momentary dopamine hit. That bigger vision is everything. To give up something, we have to love something else more.

I'm acting this out right now, as a matter of fact. I'm alone on my laptop, writing these words. Honestly, it's difficult and not immediately rewarding. I could open up my Internet browser and do something far easier. I could avail myself of some supernormal stimuli.

But I want something else even more. I want a lot of things even more, actually. In no particular order:

1. I want my words to add value to your life. That can't happen if I don't focus.

2. I want to get this book done. My publisher would prefer this as well.

3. I want to have integrity. I want what I write for you to match what I'm doing in my private life. I want to engage with God without a dark cloud of hypocrisy or shame hovering over me.

4. I want to honor my wife. I want to be a man she is proud of. I want to desire my wife and enjoy a great sex life with a real woman, the one who, in turn, calls me out to be a man in all facets of my life.

5. I want to be fully human, feeling things I'm supposed to feel, rather than becoming desensitized. I want to have real human reactions, not dulled responses to beauty or transcendence.

6. I want to be a man who is entirely present, ready to respond wisely, seeing things through clear eyes.

7. I want to be energized. I want to be strong—at least, as strong as I can be. I want to be creative. I'm at my best when I have lots of ideas. I want to have a light heart.

8. I want to look back and be satisfied that I did real things and didn't waste my ambition on soul-killing stuff.

9. I want to have the energy and curiosity and drive to be able to think about far-off places and then, you know, actually go there.

10. I'm not sure if I have a tenth thing, but it's weird to end a list at #9. (Maybe you can make up a tenth thing here: "I want _____."
There. Now you get coauthor credit. Write your name next to mine on the cover.)

The bigger vision will win. Once we see it, we have to do whatever it takes to make it possible. This is not about guilting ourselves into obedience; it's about getting a glimpse of something beautiful.

Forgive me for not sounding like the usual man-book author here, but the "something beautiful" in this case is you: Your life lived in the fullness of your Creator's intent. You being maximally you, instead of being dragged into the muck of the surrounding culture.

It's God's desire that you live truly unencumbered, truly free. Not "free" to enslave yourself, but free to be the you we all need you to be.

A Tale of Two Men, and Every Single Woman

There's a video of this. You can look it up.[1] And you really should, because rarely do we men get such a vision of our two possible futures so beautifully and starkly laid before us.

There are two men in the video, which was taken on someone's phone on a street in France.

Guy #1: An immigrant from Mali. We can't see his face. What we see is him boldly scaling a building. Why is he scaling a building? He sees a child dangling from a high balcony, so he attacks the problem. He uses every bit of his strength and endurance and successfully rescues the little four-year-old boy.

Guy #2: The four-year-old's dad. Oh, wait. He's not in the video. He's nowhere to be seen. Why is he nowhere to be seen while his child's life hangs in the balance?

He wasn't paying attention. He was playing Pokémon.

Remember this and take it to heart: Every single woman in the world admires Guy #1. Every single woman thinks that what he did is very, very attractive.

What does he look like? We can't tell. Doesn't matter.

What kind of car does he drive? Again, doesn't matter.

How ripped are his abs? No one cares. He's attractive because of what he's doing.

Also remember this: Every single woman in the world thinks Guy #2 is a loser who needs to grow up.

Why? Because every single woman loves a man who takes responsibility. Guy #2 doesn't take responsibility.

Guy #1 takes responsibility not only for himself but for someone he doesn't even know. Again, *taking responsibility is the very essence of masculinity.*

In Jesus, we get a brilliant example of masculinity. (We'll talk later about Jesus' master class on how to treat women.) Jesus is described as the second Adam, the one we need who takes responsibility for the world. He's the absolute opposite of passive.

To recap:

Every single woman loves a man who actually does real things in real life.

She is not impressed by a man who rescues an entire virtual division in *Call of Duty.*

She is very impressed by a man who is willing to risk his own life for the right cause.

Every single woman loves a man who rises above the crowd of do-nothings. Guy #1 does this literally, of course. But think about it. He wasn't the only one who saw that kid dangling. He was just the only one who said, "I'm fixing this."

"But Brant," you say. "These are really big blanket statements. 'Every single woman . . .'? Really? You can't say that!"

"But this is my book, and I totally can," I reply. "Yes, there is probably one woman who hates men who rescue children, and yes, she will leave a bitter review of this awesome book on Amazon, but I'm saying it anyway."

And here's another big blanket statement that's worth remembering for the rest of your life: *A man whose primary "heroism" is virtual is not the man he could have been.*

You can be Guy #1 or Guy #2.

No one can make that decision for you.

It's your call.

About Video Games

I Love Them, and They're Just Too Awesome

No, seriously, I mean it. Video games are too awesome.

Let me tell you that back in the day, Atari made a "football" game. Honestly, the only way we knew it was a football game was because the label on the cartridge said "Football" and there was a drawing of football players on it.

The actual game bore no resemblance to the label, or to football, or to sports, or to life on earth. The "field" was vertical, and you could see all one hundred yards at once. Each "team" had four apparently frozen robots that slid around in lockstep. The "ball" was square, and it was one (1) giant pixel.

The playbooks encompassed two (2) whole plays. There were no player names, no customizations, no varying levels. Just robots moving in unison, with an off-screen "crowd" making a strange grinding noise.

The Atari football game was primitive, repetitive, juvenile, pathetic, and ridiculous.

So I played that thing for 4,506,201 hours.

And not because I was a kid either. I could still play it for hours in one sitting if given the chance. Long after everyone else has tapped out, I can keep playing video games.

This is why I stay away from immersive RPG-type hobbies. Not because role-playing games are inherently evil but because they're simply too *fun* for me. I'm not kidding about this.

I call video games "awesome," and I use that word a lot. Of course, it means "super great" or "amazing" in the usual sense. But it's from the word "awe," so it also means inspiring fear or apprehension. When it comes to video games, I mean "awesome" in both senses.

I'm fearful of losing my life to those things.

My day-to-day, seemingly mundane real life can't compete with gaming. Gaming is another form of supernormal stimuli and can make me lose my taste for real things.

But I've made a commitment to living a real life. This is part of my arrangement with God. He's given me one life, and I'm going to be loyal to him. He wants me to be fully me and fully present. He put me here, and no one else has the exact same circumstances. No one else is around the exact same people. I have a role to play, and I need to show up for it. He's given me a garden to keep, and I'm going to keep it.

> My day-to-day, seemingly mundane real life can't compete with gaming.

Real life is at a distinct disadvantage because it doesn't always seem to pay off. In games, I know if I collect enough whatever-points or kill all the characters on a particular level, I will level up. There's a fairly immediate win in games that doesn't often happen in reality.

I can have (seeming) adventures without any of the mundane work. If I pop in a military game, I skip right past all the real work of becoming a soldier. Suddenly I'm a Navy SEAL without doing a single push-up or half-drowning in a freezing ocean during training. I can use advanced weaponry without ever learning a thing about it. It's tough for reality to compete with that.

For a lot of us, video games can make the rest of life pale and boring. They consistently provide a dopamine hit, so our brains become hyper-reactive to it, which dulls our appreciation of the rest of life.

Maybe we used to enjoy taking a long walk with our dog, but now we don't because we just want to get back to our game. The rest of life is just something to put up with until we can be with our precious game again. We become like Gollum in the cave with his ring. (A friend of mine finally quit a strategy game he was playing when he realized he was thinking about it all the time, even while sitting in his law classes. He nearly failed before he thought, *You know, maybe this is a problem if my game is more important than law school.*)

Look, just like our discussion about disordered lust, this isn't a guilt trip. It's all very understandable. I've been there. But I'm confident the real you—the one who has hopes and dreams and longs to find out what you can be—doesn't want to trade in reality for fake life. I'm confident you don't want to trade in real accomplishment for fake accomplishment. And that is because I'm confident of the very thesis of this book, that men are actually designed *for* something, and that something isn't random. You are created purposefully, so not fulfilling that purpose isn't just an opportunity missed, it's a tragedy, and you and the people who love you can sense it.

I just saw a photo of a thirty-four-year-old man named Ikuo. He's a normal-looking guy in a white T-shirt. The photo was taken in his room, which makes sense because Ikuo hadn't left his room in seven years. The photo was published on the National Geographic website as part of a story on a growing trend in Japan.

Known as *hikikomori*, these are people, mainly men, who haven't participated in society or shown a desire to do so for at least a year. They rely instead on their parents to take care of them. In 2016, the Japanese government census put the figure at 540,000 for people aged fifteen to thirty-nine.[1] But it could easily be double that number. Since many prefer to stay entirely hidden, they remain uncounted.[2]

The *hikikomori* phenomenon isn't limited to Japan. People are increasingly shutting themselves out of real life and choosing to live their entire lives online. I'm convinced that as technology advances, this is a trend that will only increase.

(Movie idea: a dystopian future where only a few people resist living virtual lives out of a conviction that living in truth inherently matters. I'm sure it's been done. My other movie idea is a reboot of *Gladiator*, starring Joaquin Phoenix as Commodus, with all the other roles filled by Muppets. Ridley Scott, if you're reading this, call me.)

Back to the point. Please don't reduce this chapter to a simple rule: "He says don't play video games" or "He says video games are evil." That sort of reductionism can provide us an excuse, a justification to keep the status quo, but I'm challenging you to question what's really at stake.

As someone who loves gaming, I've had to wrestle with these questions:

If God created me, he had a purpose in mind. Was it for me to spend my days in unreality?

If the unnatural dopamine hits are altering my brain, rendering the rest of life bland and colorless in comparison to games, is that a problem?

If God has placed me in a certain context with certain people and certain abilities, shouldn't I be fully present in that context?

If God created me to be the answer to others' problems and a blessing to the vulnerable, how tragic would it be if I was too busy playing a character?

So I'm not giving you (or me) a no-games rule. That's not how this works. Instead, I'm trying to show you that the God of the Bible is unique. He is looking to go through life with you. There's a friendship aspect to this. He wants you and me to grow up so our desires will start to change. Then he can trust us to want the right things.

The hurting world and our hurting communities need us to solve real-world problems, protect real-world people, and fight real-world injustice. Actually, let me rephrase that a bit. The hurting world and *your* hurting community need *you* to solve real-world problems, protect real-world people, and fight real-world injustice. Please don't waste your God-given desire for adventure and accomplishment by being a fake hero fighting fake injustices in fake worlds.

> **Please don't waste your God-given desire for adventure and accomplishment by being a fake hero fighting fake injustices in fake worlds.**

Join me in reality. It's not always the most exciting here. For one thing, I've noticed there are fewer explosions, and I can't hop as high. Also, my first-person point of view is blurrier.

But when you take a deep breath and get over the dopamine addiction (and you can!), you'll see that the non-virtual reality is the reality you're perfect for.

Decision Two

Protect the Vulnerable

Your Neighborhood Should Be Safer Simply Because You're There

Dishal Sooku is a quiet guy. He works hard. He's thirty-eight years old. He likes to laugh.

One afternoon he was sitting at a table with his dad on a veranda outside the small restaurant he owns in South Africa. Dishal noticed two women and a small child, a girl. His dad noticed a "suspicious-looking guy" nearby and told Dishal to keep an eye on him.

That's when the guy jumped a short railing and lunged to kidnap the little girl. Little did the guy know that at that exact second, he had no chance.

Almost instantaneously—it's on video, you can watch it—Dishal is on top of the guy, throwing him to the ground and putting him in a glorious choke hold. "I saw the video again and I thought, how did I do that?" he said. "All those thoughts go through your mind. But I guess, at that moment, when I saw that little girl, everything else just took over."[1]

Dishal had years of martial arts experience. He needed it all for that one moment. He said he surprised himself that he acted so fast. He held the attacker until the police came, and the attacker was charged with attempted kidnapping.

"A big part of martial arts is that you learn to control the situation, and I think that is what happened," Dishal said. "I needed to control him so that he would let go of this child—it was a combination of awareness and training and all that."[2]

I love this guy's story, for several reasons:

1. It went viral worldwide. People hunger for a story where someone steps in to defend the vulnerable.
2. Because Dishal trained for years, he was able to do something he wouldn't have been able to do otherwise. His self-discipline made him capable of remarkable things.
3. He credits not just his training but his awareness (and his dad's awareness). He was actively looking out for the people around him.
4. And my favorite aspect: Dishal Sooku is unassuming. Little did the ladies with the young girl know that they were safer because of a quiet man at a table nearby.

The people in your neighborhood, at your school, or at your workplace should be safer because you're there. Even if they don't know it.

Just because you're in the mix, they're better off. If the world around us is our garden and we're faithful to keep it, then kids, older folks, and other vulnerable people around us are safer.

But most of them won't be aware of it. In fact, if you're a young man, they'll suspect the opposite. They'll consider you something of a threat. People have become fearful of men, particularly young ones, and that's completely understandable. A full 80 percent of the violent crimes in the US are committed by men, and men are most likely to commit a violent crime before age twenty-five.[3]

Young men are in their athletic, physical prime before age twenty-five. And it's also true that before they're twenty-five, their brains haven't fully developed. They're much more likely to take risks, including exceedingly stupid and/or entertaining ones. They're given a desire for adventure and a desire to push the envelope.

This desire isn't a bad thing, in and of itself. In fact, it's a good thing. It's to help them rise to the challenge of leaving their homes. It's to give them the drive to set out on their own, take responsibility for their lives and livelihood, and start their own families.

> **The people in your neighborhood, at your school, or at your workplace should be safer because you're there. Even if they don't know it.**

It's not there to prompt them to drive 140 miles per hour on the interstate and jeopardize people's lives.

So use your power, your athleticism, and your God-given drive to do something. Use it to defend people, not threaten them.

The other morning in my neighborhood, I walked by a young girl with a backpack. She was coming my way on the sidewalk and quickly zipped by without making eye contact.

In a different era, perhaps, I would've smiled and said hello. But I know she's likely been taught not to engage with strangers, particularly strange men. I know this because I told my daughter the very same thing. It makes sense.

But you know what? This girl is actually safer because I'm in the neighborhood, even if she doesn't know it. I will look out for her. When I've seen suspicious or abusive activity in our neighborhoods, I've physically intervened to defend the kids. Would I get pummeled in a street fight? Maybe. But that's okay.

Even if you're like me and not physically intimidating, it can be very effective to speak up. It's remarkable how quickly some people will back down if anyone—anyone at all—challenges them.

Like Dishal, we should make it a habit to be aware of what's happening around us. We should notice if someone's behaving strangely and be ready to intervene on behalf of others.

I don't want to be passive. I want to watch over people and use whatever I have to defend them. We can all do this with our applied intelligence, our words, our bodies, our money, and our lives. Whether people notice or praise us isn't the issue. We know that our Creator sees us doing exactly what he created us to do.

If the men show up, the most vulnerable aren't so vulnerable anymore.

They have us.

Lessons from Mouse Utopia

Okay, another quick question for you: What, exactly, is "Mouse Utopia"?

(A) Mid-90s band from Portland

(B) Slang term for Disney World

(C) Real-life nightmare-scape for mice that will haunt your dreams forever

Good news! The correct answer is (C)—the nightmare-scape that will haunt your dreams forever!

It was an experiment conducted in the 1960s. John B. Calhoun wanted to study the effects of overpopulation, so he set up "Universe 25," a splendid place for mice to live, with open areas and corridors and little stairs and platforms and rooms. He made sure the mice would not want for anything. He set them up with an endless, bountiful food supply. Water was always easily available. There were no predators allowed. The bedding was constantly refreshed to provide the ideal nesting environment for baby mice.

The question behind the experiment: Would this mouse society flourish? (I now realize that perhaps I've already spoiled the story, since I mentioned that part about how this will haunt your dreams forever.)

At first, there were no surprises. The mice got busy making other mice. Real busy. After a year, there were 620 mice in Mouse Utopia.

At about day 315, though, Calhoun noticed something: The population growth had slowed markedly. The mice's behavior had changed. Drastically. And it all went downhill from there.

The male mice started acting dejected and disinterested, then they got violent. They formed little groups and randomly attacked other mice.

The female mice changed too. They started abandoning their young and, in some cases, even attacked their own babies.

It became Tarantino-level violent. Mice would kill and eat each other.

Not all the mice started killing, though. Some just got really into themselves. They removed themselves entirely from all social bonds and isolated themselves on their own little platforms. They spent their lives grooming themselves, eating, and drinking. Calhoun called them "The Beautiful Ones" because they looked marvelous. They didn't have missing tails and battle scars like the others. They lived and died alone.

So, overpopulation is deadly, right? That's surely the lesson here.

Except for one very weird thing: *There was room for thousands more mice.*

The population topped out on day 600. Then it started plummeting, and the mice simply would not alter their destructive and apathetic behavior, not even when the population dropped to just a few dozen mice. They stopped breeding entirely. They just weren't interested.

A few months later—and this is the development that ensured that Pixar will never bid on the Mouse Utopia movie rights—all the mice were dead.

Think about it: The mice had everything they could want. All the space they needed, all the food and water, and no threats.

But maybe that was the problem. The male mice didn't have to do anything. They didn't have to find new food sources. They didn't have to defend their territory. They didn't have to protect anything.

And it wasn't just Universe 25 that went so wrong. Calhoun had done previous studies and found the same thing. He called it "behavioral sink," when the mice just stopped doing what they were designed to do. In a previous experiment, the mouse universe he set up had space for five thousand mice. The population in that one crested at two hundred before becoming a mouse ghost town.[1]

Obviously, there's a limit to what we can interpret from this and apply to ourselves. But the National Institute for Mental Health funded this, and they clearly thought it had some potential take-aways beyond, "See what happens when you try to give mice a cool place to live? They're ungrateful and hate you and everything else, so don't waste your time. Don't do it. Try raccoons."

Mice need purpose. How much more so for humans? We're made to *do* things, and not just any things. We intuitively sense that there's something tragic about Universe 25. There's something pitiful about creatures refusing to thrive, refusing to even summon the life force to be what they're made to be.

Comfortable, decadent human societies have disappeared in similar ways. Rome, of course, is the classic example. Before being easily taken over by Alaric and the Goths (also a cool band name idea), the Romans had stopped having babies. The western part of the empire massively depopulated. Many Romans lived on free bread from the empire, and the family structure was disappearing.

While the fall of Rome is always a fun conversation topic, this book isn't about critiquing modern society per se. It's about looking at *us*—you and me—and deciding who we really want to be.

Remember, if we are focused on our keeper-of-the-garden purpose, we're a source of life for those around us. We stay more energized. We pay attention. We are engaged. We become encouragers.

Vulnerable people feel safe around us, while people with evil motives suspect we're dangerous.

Chaos and apathy may rule outside our spheres of influence, but within them, we're still faithful and awake. While seemingly everyone else might be losing the melody of life, we'll be the ones who can still sing it.

I love what Gandalf says to Denethor (author goal: include LOTR reference in every chapter) late in *The Lord of the Rings*, when things are especially dark:

> The rule of no realm is mine, neither of Gondor nor any other, great or small. But all worthy things that are in peril as the world now stands, those are my care. And for my part, I shall not wholly fail of my task, though Gondor should perish, if anything passes through this night that can still grow fair or bear fruit and flower again in days to come. For I also am a steward. Did you not know?[2]

Yes, the culture may be going full Mouse Utopia. It may completely collapse. But if you and I can help anything pass through this night "that can still grow fair or bear fruit and flower again in days to come," we have not failed.

We have a job to do. We are stewards. Did you not know?

What You Do Actually *Matters*

People get really weird when it comes to "spiritual" matters. We start thinking and saying stuff that doesn't make any sense. Like when we see an obvious need, we might say, "If God wants that need met, he will make sure it happens." Or if someone is abusing their power in a church setting, we might say, "If God wants to resolve that situation, he will do it."

I don't want to get in a big theological debate about this, because I always get confused when it comes to theoretically unpacking God's will and our free will and whether we make real decisions and so forth. I've never had a productive discussion about it. I am but a simple man.

Yet I have noticed that when we want to start the car in the morning, we don't say, "If God wants me to get to work, he will start the car." No, because we have the keys. And most of us have hands and wrists. We can put the key in the ignition or press a button like so, and voilà—the car starts.

When I want a coffee, I put a coffee pod thing in the Keurig and turn it on. I don't usually say, with great fervency and expectation, "Lo, if God wants me to have a coffee, it is he who will put a coffee pod thing in the Keurig."

We only tend to get weird and super "spiritual" when it comes to *other* people's needs. These are things we consider God's job. This has a bonus effect of taking us off the hook. We think it doesn't matter whether we meet the need or not, because someone else will do it if God *really* wants it done.

I don't think that's true. And while it's a bit scary, perhaps, that things actually depend on us, it's also exciting, because it means something really, really important. It's something I hope you remember from this book, along with all my references to Gandalf:

What you do actually matters.

Here's what I mean. A few weeks ago in our town, a middle school girl was in a minivan that was struck by a motorcyclist going 120 miles per hour. She was killed. I believe that if the young man riding the motorcycle had not made the choice to drive recklessly, she would still be alive.

There was another recent incident here in which a woman accidentally drove her car into a canal. The car was sinking. She had almost drowned when a police officer jumped in and pulled her to safety. I believe that if he hadn't done that, she would be dead.

This sort of thing may seem obvious to you, but it's surprising how often we miss the point and wonder if what we do (or don't do) really matters. Maybe because what we do matters so much? Maybe that's what's hard to take in?

A few years ago, a man with an AK-47 intended to kill everyone on a train in France. The likely death toll, according to the investigators, would have been three hundred people. But three young men aboard decided to intervene physically. They took him down and held him in a choke hold until he was unconscious.

Did it really matter that they acted? Of course it did. But most people on the train wouldn't have made that choice. That's probably why the young men's action resulted in tears of relief and gratitude, France's highest honor, and a Clint Eastwood movie.

If you don't do something, don't just assume it will get done. Your life is deeply meaningful, one way or another. Your efforts matter. Your work matters. You're the only one uniquely placed in your position in the world. No one else is in your exact context.

If someone needs encouragement and you don't provide it, it's quite possible they will not be encouraged. If someone needs their existence acknowledged and you are in a position to do that but take a pass, it's possible no one will acknowledge it. Yes, God wants it done, and yes, he has the power to do it. That's why he put *you* there.

———

Once, I was riding in a van in a city in Senegal, Africa. Senegal is a very hot, dry place, and it was extraordinarily hot on this particular day. The streets were jammed with people shopping and selling in the heat and the exhaust of the intense traffic.

As we sat at a stoplight, I saw a tall, relatively young woman in a vivid blue dress gesturing toward us, trying to get our attention. She was carrying a bag of nuts and clearly was hoping we'd buy some. She looked distressed.

I tried to avoid eye contact with her, and the van set off when the light turned green. We stopped at the light a block farther. I looked back . . . and saw the woman in the blue dress behind us, now running to catch up. She was dodging and weaving between all the people. It was over one hundred degrees, and in the intense sunshine and through the filth of the street, she was sprinting in her long blue dress.

She had the look of true desperation. I wondered why she was so motivated to catch up to us, then it popped into my head: She had children she was determined to feed. She'd seen foreigners in a van, and foreigners usually had money. Someone might buy her peanuts!

The van pulled forward, and I looked back again. The woman was still running. I asked the driver to pull over, and he did. The woman finally caught up with us. It was so hot the heat rolled into the van as we lowered a window.

"I'll buy some peanuts," I said.

She indicated that they cost a dollar, so I handed a dollar to the person by the window. None of the other Americans in the van were interested. They weren't hungry, they said. And our van pulled away.

I watched the woman turn away and begin walking back.

I tell you this story even though I'm not sure there's anything remarkable about it. It's just one of those memories that sticks in my head, and every time I think about it, I feel something like a punch in the stomach. It's regret. You know why?

I had more cash. I gave her one lousy dollar.

She didn't make me feel guilty. She didn't ask for more. It's just that I could have given her fifty dollars, or whatever I had, and it wouldn't have hurt me in the slightest. I meet a desperate woman and give her . . . *one dollar*? This was a small moment, a quick decision for me, but it could have been incredibly significant for her.

I know God forgives me for things. But I also know what we do has consequences. What we do really matters. We have real opportunities, and we can really seize them and bring real mercy into people's lives.

Or not.

But oh, how it matters.

The Ultimate Betrayal

If I'm right (and I totally am) that true masculinity is rooted in our unique role as keepers of our personal gardens and that we are to protect and defend and help the vulnerable, then there's a flip side. *Becoming* a threat to those vulnerable people . . . is treason.

And so is passivity in the presence of threats to them.

I remember talking to a friend of mine whose kids were toddlers. You may not be surprised to learn he was tired and frustrated. He was trying to grow as a believer but also struggling to stick it out with his family. Either he had to man up and fully take responsibility, or he would leave and strand his wife and his children.

I sat in the car with him when he was dropping me off one day, and I said, "Man, in your situation, you're going to be either a hero or a scoundrel." There was really no in-between for that guy.

But then again, maybe there's no in-between for any of us.

Either we accept our roles or we don't. And that's not just a family thing. It's in how we approach everything.

As I write this, there's a story in the news about Olivia, an eight-year-old, and her little brother, RJ, who's four. They went for their first sledding outing ever and lost control. Their mom and dad could see it happening from atop the hill but couldn't do anything about it. The sled was going too fast, picking up momentum.

And then it steered straight into an icy pond.

The parents saw a fourteen-year-old boy named Kieran Foley jump into the water. He grabbed little RJ first and handed him to a friend who'd also jumped in the water. And then RJ was handed to another teenage boy . . . and another . . . and another . . . until he was safe.

Five teenage guys jumped into the freezing water and quickly made a human chain to rescue both RJ and Olivia.

"We definitely had to do something. We can't just sit there and watch," Kieran said.

"We hope that anybody would do that," fellow teenager Tyler Armagan said. "It just happened to be us there."

But "anybody" doesn't always do that. Amazingly, people *do* "just sit there and watch." It happens all the time. There's even a name for this: the bystander effect, when people stand aside and watch, even in an obvious emergency, thinking surely someone else will take care of the problem.

"What they did was, like, just amazing," RJ and Olivia's dad said.[1]

In their situation, it was obvious there was no halfway. Either they got in the water or they didn't.

In our daily lives, it may not be so obvious. If we are faithful in our protective roles, we may not be publicly recognized as heroes. And if we fail to be faithful, no one outside our homes may say a word to us. Especially because we live relatively isolated lives (compared to the rest of humanity in history), outsiders don't always see when a man is a threat to the security of his wife or children instead of being a source of their security.

Many people may not see it, but the heroism is quite real, and so is the treason.

In another chapter we'll discuss in more depth making women feel secure, but for now let's talk about the opposite: making women feel insecure.

For the women who know you—whether it's your sister, mother, neighbor, coworker, whoever—it should be unthinkable that you would harm them. And for the women who don't know you yet, you have to interact with them knowing that even your physical stature or strength can represent a threat. Women around the world and for centuries have often been at the mercy of the men around them, and it's no mystery why they can feel menaced by male behavior that's even subtly unpredictable or predatory.

In the case of marriage, whether it's because of your Adam-like passivity, your flirtation with other women, your explosive temper, or the subtle way you allow her to suspect you don't care about her . . . the word "betrayal" isn't too harsh.

Think about it. You took a vow for this woman. She pinned her hopes on you. Whether she articulated it or not, she had a vision for you as a keeper of the garden, someone she thought could rise to the occasion and be a defender of the weak. She was willing to bet her future on you. And you're going to be a threat to her? You're going to make her feel insecure instead of adding to her security? Instead of cheering her on and promoting her and helping her take on the world, you're going to undermine her?

Some guys will read this and feel guilty. I'm okay with that, provided that the guilt motivates a change. If it does, thank you for having the guts to evaluate yourself, rethink things, and decide to change. Few are willing to do that. You have my respect.

But I'm not writing this to induce guilt. I'm writing this to underscore how often it is that *we become the enemy in the garden*. Instead of watching over our garden and the precious people within it, we become the invader. We're the museum security guard who was trained and trusted to guard precious artifacts but is now smashing them on the floor.

Imagine a culture that is practically *designed* to get us to betray our role. Imagine a culture that trains us to be sources of disarray instead of calm. Imagine a culture that trains us to see women as objects to exploit or to see a commitment to our own children as optional. Imagine a culture that lulls us into becoming consumers of entertainment instead of creators of order and peace.

Imagine a culture that lacks grown men.

That culture shouldn't be hard to imagine, because it's where we live. So if you make a decision to be a keeper of the garden and a creator of order, peace, and security, you will stand out like . . . like . . . what's the phrase?

Oh yes—a man among boys.

Yes, You Should Shelter Your Children

Another quick quiz:

If you have kids, should you shelter them?

- (A) What kind of question is that? Of course you should shelter your kids.
- (B) There is no B.
- (C) Why are you still reading this quiz? The correct answer is A.
- (D) Seriously.

It's your *job* to shelter your kids.

When my kids were growing up, there were shows I wouldn't let them watch. "You shelter your kids," people told me, like it was an allegation of wrongdoing or maybe was a little suspicious.

My response: "Right. Yes. I shelter my kids. That's a thing I do."

A good father provides shelter—physically, emotionally, psychologically, and spiritually.

If you're a wise father who loves your children, you will shelter them. You will protect them. You will shield them. You will filter the world for them. You will do your best to know what and who is influencing them, even if it means inconvenience to you or feeling like you're the only parent on the block who might care.

They are vulnerable, and they have you to defend them. You are the keeper, and in your garden, these are the most delicate little plants.

As they grow, yes, you begin to hand over more and more freedom, and you talk to them about more abstract and difficult parts of modern life. But this is still a form of sheltering. You are still there with them, still involved in their lives.

You must know them well. You must know who they are and who they can become.

One of the classic *Saturday Night Live* sketches featured the late comedian Sam Kinison (who was known for hysterical screaming) as a preschool teacher. A happy mom and dad walk in for their very first parent-teacher conference about their well-behaved little girl. But the teacher tells them their daughter has serious problems.

Why? How? They can't believe it.

He shows them a picture she drew of a happy little house and a smiley-face sun in the sky. "See this? This is insane!"

They don't get it, so he walks them over to a classroom window. "Look at the sun up there. Can you see what that is? Can you settle a bet for me? Do you see a 'smiley face' on there? YES OR NO???"

He then launches into a screaming tirade about sheltered preschoolers reading books like *The Little Engine That Could* instead of his gruesome war tome about "six guys trapped in Vietnam."[1]

The real world, right? Get those kids exposed right now, as if there's not a season for everything. As if childhood isn't fit for children. As if sheltering isn't one of the things you are precisely charged with doing as a parent.

You can take a kid to a thousand lessons and offer them the finest tutors, but that's not the objective of a parent. Your main task here is not to impart skills. You do not exist to make your kids marketable to the corporate world. You are here to shape character as securely and fully as you can before they leave your home.

While my wife and I were sheltering our children, our goal was to create adults who could take on the world. We've always wanted them to know God and be on mission for him, wherever and whatever the cost.

But that doesn't mean they should be "missionaries" as children. Childhood is their time to be protected and formed, not sent into battle. It's the time a great protector and gardener will use to allow the precious seedlings to take root.

"But," you might counter, "can't you take sheltering too far?" Of course you can. You could move off the grid and cut your kids off from relationships with other kids, or intervene to try to protect them from ever experiencing defeat or disappointment.

> **You do not exist to make your kids marketable to the corporate world. You are here to shape character as securely and fully as you can before they leave your home.**

But you know what? I honestly don't see much overprotecting. What I do see is a toxic and pervasive pop culture—a mix of consumerism, sex, violence, and overstimulation that even adults can't handle.

Yes, we want kids to be secure, confident adults. So here's the idea: *Do* show your kids the "real world," unmediated by pop culture. Show them the real world in time, in season, and informed by wisdom. Help them to understand from the outset that some things aren't appropriate for them now but will be in time. If you can afford it, take them out of the country to the developing world. Give them lots of great (usually not modern) books. Gradually give them more and more latitude as they demonstrate their own wisdom, with the goal of producing well-formed, free-thinking, independent adults by their late teens.

As I mentioned, you'll actually have to know your kids. Really know them. This may mean giving up your awesome car or house and getting a less lucrative job in exchange for time. It may mean changing your own media choices and shutting off the flow of pop culture into your life.

Yes, it's hard. That's the problem with helping people grow up: We have to be grown-ups.

I remember watching the Batman movie *The Dark Knight* in the theater, sitting two seats from a guy and presumably his son, who looked to be around four years old. The movie was violent and upsetting. The boy threw his face into his dad's chest, then got down and climbed under the seats. Anything to get away from the onslaught. The dad certainly couldn't be accused of sheltering, right? But was his son experiencing the "real world"?

Our culture is polluted. We know that. And we know kids are the most vulnerable to the pollution. If my kids have asthma, you can bet I'm not going to pump deadly exhaust directly into their faces.

> Yes, it's hard. That's the problem with helping people grow up: We have to be grown-ups.

I've had discussions with dads who let their kids watch sex scenes in movies, and I get a response along the lines of, "But I saw stuff like that when I was younger, and I turned out okay."

But . . . did you? Are you entirely sure you're "okay"? I wouldn't say I am. I think we're all messed up for a lot of reasons.

I once talked to a ten-year-old boy who was in tears as he told me he wished he could unsee the things he'd seen online. Before the advent of smartphones, an eighth-grade boy told me he was often left home alone and was addicted to pornography. He asked his parents to take his computer away or somehow protect him from it. They wouldn't do it.

It's rare that your kid will actually ask you to shelter them. But they still want it.

They'll rarely say, "Don't let me watch this" or "Don't let me have that." Especially when other kids get to watch this and have that.

But they're not the dad. You are. You have to make some tough calls, like whether your kid gets a smartphone. The default answer is "of course," but given the troubling connection of smartphones and the spike in teen depression and suicide, that default answer is tragic.[2]

A very wise counselor friend of mine put it another way. After observing his own kids and the young people he works with in his practice, he said the correct answer to the question, "When should I get my child a smartphone?" is "Whenever you want their childhood to end."

Your kid gets just one childhood, and they get just one you to protect it.

Setting the Tone for the Vulnerable in Your Home

Someone jumped on a Facebook group page and asked a question about an enormously hot-button issue. He wanted to know what people thought.

Remember, this was a Facebook comment thread, where common sense and courtesy go to die. I knew that the hundreds of people in the group had wildly varying opinions on said incendiary issue.

Usually, a post on this particular page might gather four or five comments. This one already had ninety-one. I almost couldn't bear to look. I knew how it would go: utter bedlam, chaos, and hatred. And also some GIFs.

But for some reason I clicked. I read the comments.

They were thoughtful. Gentle, even. Respectful. Intelligent. There was genuine disagreement and genuine respect for one another, even though the people were strangers. No one went off on anyone else.

It was shocking. How was this possible?

It happened, I'm convinced, because the focal point of the Facebook group was the work of a particular late author, one who was known for his thoughtfulness, level-headedness in debate, and willingness to listen. The people in the group (including me) are fanboys and fangirls who are there because they want to be more like him, and he wanted his followers to be more like Jesus.

My takeaway: You can have a tremendous unseen effect on those around you. You can set the tone; you start the melody and others will sing along. If you think, *But that's not me—I'm not usually a leader*, please know that you absolutely *will* have this tone-setting influence if you have a family.

Your family will take their cues from you. You may have problems here and there—when someone is hitting the wrong notes—but the tenor of the home will be one you set. If you are consistently gentle and respectful with your wife, your family will tend toward gentleness and respect with each other.

If you are passive or disengaged, a measure of chaos will fill your home. Human nature will take over, as sure as weeds choking out the garden you're supposed to keep.

You can watch how this plays out in sports. Almost instantly, a new coach can radically impact a team's performance, and not just from an X's-and-O's standpoint. The entire ethos can quickly change from ragged and fractious to streamlined, peaceful, and effective simply because of the demeanor of the team's leadership and what that leadership clearly, truly values.

This is the effect you can have on your home. It's almost magical. If you're at peace, if you're growing as a believer, if you're active, present, and engaged with your family, your home atmosphere will be peaceful. Everyone will benefit.

This applies to all spheres of your life—your job; your friends; your chess club; your new band, Mouth of Gravel . . . you name it.

Imagine it like you're a composer scoring an improvisational movie. If what you write is orderly and beautiful, the actors will play their parts accordingly. If it's a crashing, unpredictable, chaotic horror soundtrack, you can bet the actors around you will play their roles in that movie too.

When I was growing up, the movie score in my home was frightening. I won't go into depth here, but I made this conscious decision one day while hiding: *If I ever get married, if I'm ever a father, I know what my kids won't have to endure. I'm going to do the opposite of what I've experienced.*

I spent much of my childhood in fear. *That won't happen when I'm a dad*, I thought. *My wife and kids will feel protected. They will feel watched over. They will feel peace in the home. There will be laughter and warmth and consistency and yet more laughter, if I have anything to say about it.*

As it turned out, that's exactly what happened. I really did get to provide my boy and girl and my wife a completely different experience. No one had to hide from me. No one had to fear what I might do next. No one had to wonder if everything was falling apart.

And lo, there was and is much laughter in the Hansen household. Thank God.

This tone-setting is essential in our protection of the vulnerable. It's not just about what we do "out there." It's about what we're creating for the people in our own home.

And those people are vulnerable, in part *because* they are in their home, the one place where they might feel like they can be themselves. The one getaway. The last redoubt. A husband/father introducing danger into the home is more than menacing. It's life-altering for everyone involved.

> **Even if you're a young man still living with your original family, start protecting the vulnerable people in your home.**

Even if you're a young man still living with your original family, start protecting the vulnerable people in your home. Your mother is vulnerable even if she's highly accomplished, confident, and strong. Same with your dad. They're not as strong as you think. People rarely are. You have weapons to hurt them, even if you've got only words.

Take care to show mercy. Practice it now. There's no reason to wait. To the extent that you can, demonstrate kindness toward your parents and your (possibly annoying) siblings. Not only is it the right thing to do, and not only will it start shaping you into a man who takes responsibility, but it will also probably kind of freak people out. So it's win-win-win.

(Bonus idea: Occasionally a friend will tell me he's considering getting his kids a dog or a cat. I almost always tell him to absolutely go for it. Having a pet gives kids something in the home more vulnerable than they are. It's a great way to teach them about mercy, about providing and protecting. It's great practice for the future. "This thing is little, and I could hurt it. But I'm not going to! I'm going to protect it.")

God created a garden, and he created humans to inhabit it. He told them to go forth and multiply. He wanted to see, and still wants to see, the whole world become more like Eden, where peace rules. It's the kind of peace that lets little things grow and flourish and blossom.

Make that the plan for your home, both now and in the future.

Set the tone. Start the melody, and make it a loving, consistent, secure one.

The Most Vulnerable Person I've Ever Met

I was "emceeing" a concert by artist Toby Mac. I am terrible at emceeing, but since I'm on the radio, people keep asking me to do it.

I don't like to yell, "How's everybody doing toniiiiiiiiiiiiiight?" because it's out of my idiom, and also because I've always wanted to say to emcees who do that, "Sir, you have a microphone. Why are you yelling?"

Anyway, I was asked to mention "cure" from the stage as part of the announcements. But I didn't know what "cure" was, so I had to ask. A woman who worked with CURE (they capitalize it) said it's a network of hospitals that provide surgeries for the most vulnerable children in the world—kids with disabilities in developing nations. These are kids whose problems could have been fixed quickly had they been born in the US, but where they live, the disabilities dominate their lives. They're considered cursed and often wind up defenseless and abused.

I was intrigued when I heard about this, and that the hospitals are very much about telling people *why* their kids were being healed. The patients and their desperate families are used to being treated as freaks and outcasts, but these hospitals are dedicated to flipping that upside down and letting them know about a God who loves them. These children aren't cursed. They matter deeply. They are not forgotten. In fact, God draws close to them.

I told the CURE staff that I'd love to see a hospital in action. They said, "Want to come to Afghanistan?"

"No, actually," I said. "Thanks."

But they talked me into it. And months later, when I arrived at the hospital, I was completely disoriented. The smell of gasoline and exhaust throughout Kabul, the sight of women in burqas bringing their children into the waiting area, the sound of many languages, and then a further disorienting question from the nursing staff: "Would you like to do kangaroo duty?"

"Uh . . . yes?" I said. "I mean, I haven't spent much time in hospitals. Does this involve hopping?"

The staff had me wash up and then took me to a neonatal intensive care unit. I sat down in a rocking chair. They had me unbutton a couple top buttons of my shirt. Then they handed me a person.

A very, very, very small person.

A one-pound person.

They said her family name was Zakara—she hadn't been given a first name yet, since her family didn't expect her to make it. And could I please hold her? She had been very sick. But she needed to make skin contact with someone.

So that's kangaroo duty, apparently. I sat there holding this tiniest of persons to my chest. I didn't know humans could be that small. She would grab my finger and then look up at me. She wanted to make eye contact.

People in the room eventually filed out, and it was just this tiny girl and me. I could feel her little breaths, and it seemed impossible that someone this small could exist.

I had just landed in Afghanistan, and now it was she and I.

We rocked for an hour or two. I honestly have no idea how long. It was long enough for me to do a lot of thinking.

I thought about her and how she might be one of the world's biggest underdogs. She was premature and sick, and the doctors said she likely wouldn't live. She was from a poor family. At this point, she was nameless, because her family was waiting to see if she would make it before naming her. She was in war-torn Afghanistan, a place that has seen seemingly endless conflict since Alexander the Great. As a female, she had second-class status there and few protections from abuse.

She was a scrap of life. A little scrap of life with nearly translucent skin. She was too tiny to be real, but there she was. I was looking down at her. She was looking at me directly in the eyes and blinking.

If the kingdom of God as described in the Bible is a real thing, this "scrap of life"? She's royalty.

What prestige did she have? None. What status? None. What wealth? Zero. What had she accomplished? Absolutely nothing. But in God's economy, the first are last and the last are first.

You know what? I like that. A lot.

I like underdogs. Maybe you do too. I like a God who champions them. I like a God who turns our messed-up values system on its head. Ultimately, my liking God has no bearing on who he is, but it so happens that the God described in the Bible has a particular personality. He is a defender of widows, orphans, the poor, and tiny people like that little girl.

> **The God described in the Bible has a particular personality. He is a defender of widows, orphans, the poor, and tiny people like that little girl.**

I sat with her and rocked and thought about what kind of man I want to be. In church culture, people use the term "godly man" every so often: "We should try to be godly men," or, "Ladies, you need to find a godly man." But it's not always clear what aspect of God they're talking about.

"Ladies, find a man who is omniscient and omnipresent" is probably not what they mean. They may not even know exactly what they mean.

But surely being a godly man means being a defender of the weak. Surely it means favoring the humble, as he does. Surely it means being a father to the fatherless.

God could, of course, defend little ones like this baby by himself. But for some reason, he wants us to do it too. He wants us in on it, joining him in the work of tending his garden, caring for the little things.

It's an honor.

Maybe God wants us to do this because people like her can't do anything for us. This baby can't pay me back. She can't say nice things about me to others and enhance my status. She can't thank me. She won't even remember me. She's got absolutely nothing.

If we love people who can't pay us back, well, there's only one reason to do that: because we love God and know that's what he told us to do. Maybe it's how he wants to be worshiped.

As this little girl and I sat there, I thought about little sparrows and how Jesus said God notices when just one of them falls. He cares. I thought about this little sparrow tucked away in northeastern Afghanistan, and I decided that if she's that important to God, then she needs to be that important to me too. (And good news: The little girl survived. I got to play with her at the hospital on one of my return visits a couple years later!)

I've since met hundreds of other patients at the CURE hospitals around the world. This has been my work and the focus of my giving for years, both in energy and in money. I've gotten to play a role in the healing of thousands of kids with correctable disabilities.

But please, please know I'm not writing this for applause. I'm telling you this because I'm so deeply thankful I get to be part of it.

I'm also telling you this because I want you to think about how *you* might be a protector of the vulnerable no matter who you are or where you're from, using whatever gifts you have.

I'm not a surgeon. I'm not a firefighter. I'm not a military guy. I'm not rich. I'm from a tiny town in Illinois. I'm on the autism spectrum. I'm from a broken home. But I use whatever gifts I have to bring mercy to children and their desperate families, and I can't stop being thankful for it and energized by it.

God is allowing me to do this. I didn't plan it out, which is why it's especially astonishing to me. I'm not a big visionary. I do ask God to help me every day, to give me the right words, to help me add value to people's lives.

You and I don't have to fit the stereotypes of what manly men look or sound like. What we do need to do is use whatever we have as great keepers of the garden to defend the defenseless.

> You and I don't have to fit the stereotypes of what manly men look or sound like. What we do need to do is use whatever we have as great keepers of the garden to defend the defenseless.

You can do this even if you're working the most seemingly meaningless job. You can give to an organization that accomplishes your mission (it certainly doesn't have to be CURE; there are a lot of great ones), and instantly—*bam*—your work takes on more meaning. You're not just detailing cars, for instance; you're using your skills and hard work to help heal a teenage girl in Malawi who's never walked before. And all the people around her will see her go from crying to dancing. They'll see an advance trailer of heaven.

Speaking of heaven . . . maybe that girl and her crying-with-joy family will get to thank you personally someday.

That car-detailing job is an important one, no? Now you're a rescuer.

Decision Three

Be Ambitious about the Right Things

Reality Is What Hits You When You're Wrong

You know how you think of just the thing to say, but it's right after when you had the chance to say it?

I had the opposite happen for the first time the other day. I actually said the right thing, right on time, and lo, it was super cool. I felt suave. It was a first, and it felt great.

I had a short Uber ride to a restaurant. The driver was a very outgoing, middle-aged guy from New York. Somehow, we went into deep conversation nearly immediately. We talked about forgiveness and anger and recognizing our own ability to justify whatever we want. I loved talking with him.

As he dropped me off, I opened the back door and started to get out. He said, "Hey, wait a second. Just curious what you think about this: Can we even really know what reality is? What if we're just imagining things? That's my question. I mean, what is reality?"

Pretty deep question. I stood there with the door open, ducking just enough to look at him. "Reality," I said, "is what hits you when you're wrong."

He paused and then laughed. "Wow . . . that's so true. Wow. Thanks, man!"

I nodded with a knowing smile, waved, shut the door, and walked off like . . . well, like super-cool guys who say cool stuff walk off.

This seriously happened. I'm going to remember it forever because it was so completely drop-the-mic-y. I'll also remember it forever because it will never, ever happen again.

The thing is, I'd just heard Dallas Willard say those words in a podcast an hour before. So there's that. I didn't feel like I had time to attribute, but if you're reading this, Uber guy, please know I totally stole that from Dallas Willard.

———

Here's an even less inspiring story. Years ago, I forgot my keys.

Now, it's also true that I forgot my keys today. And yesterday. But this particular forgetting-of-the-keys took place after an event in a large church building with a long hallway.

When I realized I'd forgotten my keys, I remembered they were upstairs in the kitchen. I was proud of myself for remembering. I quickly walked down the long, dimly lit hallway, saw a skinny post right in the middle, and walked to the left of it. No problem.

I went up the stairs, found my keys, and jogged back down, then started flat-out running. I saw the post. I did not hit the post. That would be silly. Instead, I once again went to the left of it, this time at full speed.

I smashed into a glass wall. With my face. While I was sprinting.

The wall had wire mesh in it, and it shattered where my head bashed into it. It also shattered where my knee bashed into it. And also where my hand punched it.

Somehow I stayed sort of conscious. I just bounced off the glass and stood there. Some people came running, wondering what the *boom* was. They found me dazed. And bleeding a lot. They told me later that I'd said, "I'm so sorry. I think I broke a wall." And then they hustled me off to the emergency room.

I tell you this ridiculous story because I want you to know that we don't get to construct reality. Reality did not bend to my beliefs. I bounced off reality.

Reality was what hit me when I was, you know . . . wrong.

Yes, I was intellectually convinced that there was nothing in the way of my path. That's why I was running. I was truly sincere. I was 100 percent committed. What I wanted—to simply run to the front door—was very innocent and would hurt no one.

But what I wanted didn't change reality. *My sincerity did not change reality.*

Jesus talks about the kingdom of God as the deepest reality. It's worth trading everything else for. It's worth more than all the power or prestige or money we can have in the moment. Because it's everlasting and it recognizes the true King, it's more real than anything else.

Jesus said if we put his words into practice, we're like a man who builds his house on a rock. When storms hit, his place is fine. But if we don't put Jesus' words into practice, we're like a man who builds his house on sand. When storms hit, it's game over.

Was the one who built his house on sand convinced it would last? Of course he was. Otherwise, why make the investment of time and energy? But the house collapsed anyway, because reality is what hits you when . . . you know.

If you are ambitious about the wrong things, you will be hit good and hard by reality. I just talked to a friend this morning who wishes he could go back to the time when his kids were young, get his priorities straight, and value time with them more than work. But he can't.

The key is to ask for wisdom. Wisdom means knowing what matters and what doesn't, or what matters more and what matters less. You don't want to go through life without it. It's the difference between a life of meaning and one of meaninglessness.

We should talk about that, so . . .

If You Feel Meaningless, It Might Be Because You're Investing Time and Energy in Meaningless Things

Mark this down: You will struggle with feeling meaningless when you choose to invest your time and energy in meaningless things.

This is as sure as gravity. I know it from personal experience, and lots of it.

By the way, I'm not talking about your work. Your work is not meaningless. As we'll discuss shortly, even if your job seems trivial, it's not. It matters to others, it matters to God, and it should matter very much to you.

What I'm talking about are things that don't add value to anyone's life. We are created to add value to things. When we are at our best, that's exactly what we're doing. We're making things, we're changing things, and we're improving conditions and situations for the people around us—those for whom we take responsibility.

If I'm engaged only in activities and projects that ultimately yield nothing, I will feel it. If I want to play video games all day, I can. And you know what? I'll enjoy it while I'm doing it. But there will be a psychological price to pay at the end of that day.

Over the course of time, if I'm spending significant time entertaining myself, I'll begin to feel ennui, which is a perfect word because (1) it's French, so perhaps you will think I'm cultured, and (2) it means listlessness and dissatisfaction that come from not being occupied with anything that matters.

If you are not mission focused, you will feel ennui. Millions of men do, and I've certainly felt it. But I'm telling you, it's directly related to what I'm watching and doing and where I'm putting my attention.

It's tough to exist in our culture and not deal with ennui. This is in part due to our affluence. We don't tend to struggle for food or shelter anymore. Most of us don't wake up with a start, thinking, *I've got to hunt or we will starve soon.*

I wouldn't want to live that way, though I have to admit, ennui would certainly not be an issue. But that's the way most humans have lived for millennia. They were part of communities, villages, and tribes that were motivated to work together for survival, which was always an imminent issue. But in an affluent, entertainment-driven culture, our experience is wildly different. We're living in Mouse Utopia.

It's not a coincidence that the book expressing meaninglessness so profoundly in the Bible, Ecclesiastes, was written by the richest man in the Bible, Solomon.

In order to avoid falling into the pervasive sense of meaninglessness of our culture, I have to keep my mission in front of me, reminding myself again and again that I'm to be a keeper of the garden. I'm here to protect the vulnerable, heal the sick, and be a voice of peace in my anxious town and this anxious world. I'm here to re-create and add beauty and cultivate and defend and, hopefully, add value to the lives of those around me.

Honestly, the last two days are a perfect example of me *not* being focused. I've been putting off writing. (I once heard someone say, "A real writer is someone who spends their time avoiding writing," so I totally qualify, at least on that level.) Yesterday I did the basic stuff: taking care of the dog, getting some batteries and things at the store. And I played lots of FIFA on the PlayStation. Lots. Way too much. I did very little meaningful work. All FIFA.

At the end of the day, I was listless. Surprise!

Today I got up early and forced myself to write this. I'm thinking of you as I type. I want you to know how important it is to be mission driven. I don't want you to become like so many other men who are lifeless shells of who they should be and who we need them to be.

And I'm feeling way less listless. I'm even energized. I'm doing my thing, and I'm motivated by wanting to serve you. I'm also motivated by this: If you take the approach to manhood I've shared in this book, the women and children and men around you will be the beneficiaries.

> **I've noticed that people who are actively serving others don't really struggle with feeling meaningless.**

I've noticed that people who are actively serving others don't really struggle with feeling meaningless.

This is a lesson I keep learning: My life isn't a highlight reel or Instagram feed. It's how I actually spend my days. If I fill my days with purpose, I tend to be less tired and more invigorated. If I don't, I start questioning everything and grow depressed.

If you pay attention to things that help you keep the garden around you, you'll absolutely feel less ennui. I promise.

I now know that my investments yield a return. If I pursue my own entertainment at every turn, I shouldn't be shocked when my own mental health suffers. I wasn't created for entertainment. But if I invest in what matters—adding value to the lives of others—I will come alive.

Invest in meaningless things and you'll yield meaninglessness. You'll also yield a vague, low-lying-but-quite-real anger at yourself. You may not be able to pin down why you feel that way, but the anger is there. It will come out in all sorts of ways. You'll be easily aggravated and less patient. You'll be more judgmental of the people you don't like and more prone to jealousy and bitterness.

Everything we choose to pay attention to is ultimately life-giving or ennui-giving.

This isn't to say never watch a movie or play a game. It's just that the fun thing is often the easy thing, and over time, it's a trap. We wind up off mission and frustrated at ourselves and the world, our energy drained from us. We don't have to wonder why.

We also wind up very, very boring. Be ready for that too.

Right now I'm energized. It's because I made myself do my thing.

Funny how that works.

Women Care about This a Lot, FYI

In a sense, this whole book is about being ambitious for the right things. But here's an advance warning: People rarely applaud for the right things. You may not get much feedback at all.

Do something dumb or selfish and you can win fans. Do something self-controlled and honorable and it's likely no one will notice. The strength of humility is not often celebrated.

If, say, you offer consistent extreme takes on Twitter, you can build a fan base. Echo someone's anger and they will quickly retweet you. You'll make some enemies, but you can also get tremendous positive feedback from your tribe. It's an ego stroke, and we tend to gravitate to where our egos are stroked.

Few people will cheer you for keeping perspective. Few people will cheer you for being self-controlled. You'll likely never get a comment praising you for not responding. You'll never get an Instagram comment that says, "Way to help people behind the scenes without us knowing about it!"

So many of the most praiseworthy things don't get praised, so it can be hard to stay focused. But what you're ambitious about makes all the difference.

If or when you're married, your wife will need you to be ambitious. By "ambitious," I don't mean being driven to be a billionaire, climbing a corporate ladder, buying a big house, or going in the first round of the NBA draft, although there's nothing inherently wrong with any of those things. I mean simply that your wife will ultimately respect you when she sees you have a drive to get things done. Productive things. Keeper-of-the-garden things. She'll need you to have a drive to do what's right and a motivation to protect her and your family.

> **Your wife will ultimately respect you when she sees you have a drive to get things done.**

She'll be impressed when you do things in real life. You know, non-video-game things. Even personal-record *Call of Duty* scores are not as attractive as actually doing real things. (Ask me how I know this.)

This is not just about making money. I know two guys whose wives make lots of money, and both men stay home and don't have jobs. One is very respected by his wife, and the other one isn't.

The first one attacks his responsibilities. He takes care of his wife and supervises the education of their daughters. He works on myriad projects. He doesn't tend to waste time. He gets things done for other people. He's a leader. He remains ambitious.

The other one does pretty much nothing. He stays home while the kids go to school. He comes up with excuses why he can't get a job or really do anything helpful. Not only does his wife not respect him; I'm pretty sure no one does.

Look, your wife will *want* to respect you. She'll *want* to admire you. But she won't be able to if you aren't actively making her and her home more secure.

Your wife may make more money than you. That could be threatening, but you don't need to be threatened *if* you remain engaged and forward-moving about things that have deep value. Maybe she makes good money working at a bank, and you make much less while running a Boys & Girls Club for at-risk kids or while working as a police officer. She'll still respect you if you're driven to accomplish things that matter and work with determination and passion.

If you become lazy, apathetic, or unwilling to work hard for the family or others, she'll sense that you're not fulfilling your mission. And she'll be right.

Do not underrate this factor in women's attraction to men. In fact, to most women, a man with enthusiastic purpose who isn't rich is far more attractive than a lazy, purposeless man who happens to have money. Ask them.

Of course, disordered ambition is destructive. Working eighteen-hour days to try to buy a high-end motorcycle is ambition of a sort, perhaps, but it may not make a wife feel more secure.

> **To most women, a man with enthusiastic purpose who isn't rich is far more attractive than a lazy, purposeless man who happens to have money.**

Here's another example. When I was first married, I was a lead singer in a rock band. We were pretty good, even if—in the precise words of one record company executive—I had "the stage presence of a sponge on a stick." (I'm not making that up. I still laugh about it.)

We would practice once or twice a week, and we played gigs every few weeks or so. Sometimes we'd play late nights in restaurants and bars; sometimes we'd play at music festivals or for church youth groups. The band seemed to be taking off.

Carolyn was agitated with me. I really couldn't understand why. I wasn't gone that much, the guys I was playing with were good guys, and I never flirted with women at gigs or anything.

It took me a while to get it. She was unsettled that the band might become my main thing. We hadn't been married long enough for her to know conclusively that I wouldn't let that happen. The band was actually something of a threat to her.

Now that we've been married for decades, she'd be fine with me playing in a band. (Please play with me in a band. Thanks. Wait, what's that? You want to name the band Sponge on a Stick? YOU ARE A GENIUS.) If I had, in fact, begun traveling extensively in hopes of being some kind of rock star, leaving my wife behind, it would have been ambition of a kind, certainly. But it would have been disordered ambition, pulling me toward applause and distracting me from my role as keeper of the garden. I'd be hurting my wife.

Rightly ordered ambition is a very good thing. These are the underlying questions:

Am I making her feel more secure?

Do my actions indicate that I'm willing to do what it takes to be here for her and for our kids?

Does she sense that I'm engaged with real life, ready to do what might need to be done for her?

In the garden I'm to watch over, my wife is the most beautiful flower. I want her to bloom, and rightly placed ambition will give her room to flourish.

How to Be Incredibly Awesome and Somehow Less Attractive to Women

It's true: Women think risky guys are attractive!

. . . Until they think we're stupid.

At first, if you're a risky, "dangerous" guy, you have a quality about you that's promising. Maybe you're a talented motorcycle racer, an awesome cliff diver, or a bull-riding rodeo enthusiast. It's all very cool.

Until it's not.

So when does this risk-taking make the jump from wildly attractive to stupid? When a woman trusts you with her future. When she needs you. And if you have a kid, this unnecessary risk-taking goes from being highly attractive to the exact opposite. You're actually *less* attractive to her if you're taking dumb risks.

This is because the original attraction was based on who she thought you *might* be: someone who will do what it takes to defend and provide for those around you. Your seeming bravery suggests to her that you're likely to rise to the occasion to fend off threats and ensure long-term stability.

But when your wife is taking care of three little kids while you're risking life and limb purely for the rush of it, you may find she doesn't think your hobby makes you hot anymore. "But you used to think it was hot," you might say. "You used to like it. You've changed, not me."

Unwittingly, you've revealed the problem: Yes, you didn't change, but you needed to. You needed to go from Seems-Like-He'll-Be-a-Good-Provider-and-Protector Guy to Actual-Good-Provider-and-Protector Guy.

Your cool hobby is now a threat to your wife's long-term security. This is why it's no longer sexy.

As a married father, I've taken some risks. For example, I've now been to Afghanistan multiple times, staying in Kabul neighborhoods, and each time was a significant risk. The only reason my wife was proud of me rather than disgusted was because the trips were for a purpose. I used my given platform, applying whatever skills I have, to highlight the work of the CURE hospital that served Afghan women and children.

Each time, my wife and I had to talk at length, weigh out whether the trip was worth it, and arrive at a decision together. We both realized that while the trips were somewhat dangerous, they were to protect and defend the vulnerable.

Do I kind of enjoy the excitement of a unique, on-the-edge experience? Yes. There's something to that. But if it's just for my thrills, well, that wouldn't fly with the mother of my children, nor should it.

I just read a story about a young man who wants to be a You-Tube star. He got someone to record him as he stood at the top of the Pennybacker Bridge in Austin, Texas, and then jumped into the Colorado River. Someone watching him do it called 911, and he was rescued after fracturing his skull.

His comment later: "You might see it as jumping for views. I see more. . . . I don't settle for less. I will leave my mark on this planet."[1]

Okay. But do you really want to leave it with your skull?

Was the jump dangerous? Yes. Was it attractive to females? Probably not. Why? There was no point, other than ego.

Purposeless, just-for-the-rush risk? Grow out of it.

Risks in defense of others? Oh yes, you're absolutely made for that. Go for it full-bore.

It's really not complex. I'm sure you got the point when I started this chapter, but I thought I'd keep going because I love this point so much.

Run through fire to prove you're a man? You're not a man.

Run through fire to save a baby? Now you're talking.

Ambition and Work

Even Terrible Jobs Are Great

Now, let's talk about your job. It's wonderful. Even if it's terrible.

Even terrible jobs make us serve people. In fact, that's what you're being paid to do — serve people. And not just your bosses.

This is obvious if you're a server at a restaurant. But it's true of practically every single job you can imagine. You're being paid to be a help to people.

If you're stocking shelves at a grocery store, you're helping busy moms and dads gather the food they need for their families.

If you're an accountant, you're helping people navigate difficult tax laws or making it possible for your company to meet payroll for people who are depending on an income.

If you're flipping burgers, you're preparing someone's meal. Maybe a grandma. Maybe a little kid. Whoever it is you're feeding, that someone is incredibly important to God.

Would you be doing any of those things if you didn't get paid? Probably not. But that doesn't diminish the reality that you're serving people and that your efforts are adding value to people's lives. That's a very healthy thing.

There's a famous story of two men in late middle age at a construction site. When asked, "What are you doing?" the first man says, "I'm stacking some blocks on top of each other." The second one, who's doing the exact same task, says, "I'm building a marvelous cathedral that will stand for centuries and inspire all who see it."

Sure, you can say, "I'm making a stupid ice cream cone at McDonald's." Or you can view it as fashioning something delightful, and even a little merciful, for a seven-year-old boy who just had an embarrassing day on a soccer field.

You can say, "I'm just mopping a dirty floor." Or you can say, "I'm keeping this residential center clean because without this work, this place would become disease-ridden for its patients, who already struggle with so much."

You can say, "I'm cleaning up poop in a horse barn. This is the worst." Or you can be aware that if you don't, the horses' hooves and even their lungs will soon suffer.

> **So often our "menial" jobs are vitally important works of mercy.**

So often our "menial" jobs are vitally important works of mercy.

I'm naturally a little lazy and a lot selfish. Every job I've ever had, from working in a factory to working in fields to mopping floors, has forced me out of my usual pattern and forced me to be a blessing to people.

Never look down on your job. Serving people is not humiliating. It's ennobling.

Work is a very good thing. It's not a punishment from God. It's not the result of the fall of man. It was part of the perfection of Eden before the fall. God gave Adam a job to do from the very beginning. We need work to thrive, and almost all work is meaningful. Be thankful for it.

Work is such a part of us that most of our hobbies are actually work. My main hobby (nerd alert) for years was the tabulation and organization of baseball statistics. I was essentially doing mathematical and actuarial work, coming up with algorithms and probabilities. Some people garden. Some people hunt. Some people knit or do woodworking. I have a friend who loves to find scrap wood in dumpsters and make furniture from it.

We're so made for work, we can't stop. Even most video games are essentially about performing tasks and accomplishing virtual work.

If we *do* try to stop, we start to go crazy. I'm serious about this. Watch some documentaries about retired athletes or people who win the lottery and retire early. They're not healthy. They thought they could just lie on the beach, but that's not what we're designed for. We can't do that and thrive.

If I have a regret about all the seemingly boring jobs I've had, it's that I didn't bring all my energy to them. They were repetitive and tiring, sure. I'd come home listless and worn-out. But the solution to being listless isn't always taking a vacation. The solution is bringing passion to the job.

One of my favorite comedians, Brian Regan, tells a story about working at a Walmart-type store. One day on the job, one of his coworkers excitedly whispered to him, "Hey, come here. Check this out!"

He led Brian to a hole in a wall behind where they assembled the bikes, and they stood inside the wall. No one could see them in there! They could get away with not working! No one could find them! They could spend the next six hours of their shift not doing anything!

They were also standing in the dark, cramped. It was hard to breathe.

Brian asked, "Wait, why is this better than working? We're standing in a wall."

Valid point. Instead of working to avoid work, maybe just . . . work?

There's a Scripture about this:

> Whatever you do, work at it with all your heart, as working for the
> Lord, not for human masters, since you know that you will receive

an inheritance from the Lord as a reward. It is the Lord Christ you are serving. (Col. 3:23–24)

Bring your all to what you're doing. It makes the time go faster. Even better, it's an act of worship. It's what you're made to do.

Relationships Require Bravery

This is the part about ambition with regard to relationships, which, naturally, brings us to FAQ #1,214. "Brant, would you kindly illustrate what you're saying by using a proverb about oxen?"

Answer: Yes. I will do it with Proverbs 14:4.

FAQ #1,215: "Brant, FAQ #1,214 isn't actually a frequently asked question, is it? I mean, you just made it up. Be honest."

Answer: Yes, totally, but here's Proverbs 14:4.

> Where there are no oxen, the manger is empty,
>> but from the strength of an ox come abundant harvests.

In other words, if you're going to get anything done, expect a mess. You just want to keep everything clean and seemingly under your control? Beautiful. But you will accomplish nothing.

This is obvious when it comes to things like farming. There is no mess-free farming. If you want to harvest something, you better prepare to deal with manure and soil and weeds and long, hot days full of sweat.

This is also true in sports. If your primary goal as a football player is keeping your uniform immaculate, do not expect to be drafted in the first few rounds.

I've learned the same thing applies to relationships. I can't control them. People remain mysterious to me. I don't know what they're thinking. When I think I might know what they're thinking, I'm often astonished that they could think such things.

I can't keep up with everyone's moods. I find people to be remarkably inconsistent, even with their deeply held convictions.

Relationships simply aren't reducible to math. There's far more mystery in them than I'm comfortable with. This morning I had an awkward conversation with someone I don't know very well in my own neighborhood. I'd been putting it off to avoid possible conflict. After it was over, I walked away thinking I had said something the wrong way. I think this is because I actually did say something the wrong way.

The point of this: We have to rise to the occasion and take on the risk of relationships.

I knew how adept I am at offering excuses for my passive conflict avoidance. I knew I needed to grow up and embrace the risk of actually saying things that need to be said. I was nervous, but I made myself walk out the door and cross the street. I won't bore you with the details, but overall, the meeting turned out to be completely helpful. Pleasant, even.

For a lot of us, any kind of relational work feels like going over a waterfall in a white-water raft. We can't quite see what's coming or how far we're going to fall, but it has to happen. So we do it.

We like to stay in areas of our own perceived competence, and very few men feel like they're good at relationships. We're confronted with being out of control. We don't really know what to do, and very rarely does God make it obvious.

I've noticed that after any extended social interaction, my desire to play video games spikes. It becomes intense. I think this is because I so desperately want to touch base with something I can control, something I'm good at, and something that takes my mind off relational stress and requires no real risk.

Our default setting is to stay comfortable, to stay clean from the mess. That means sticking to our own areas of expertise and excusing ourselves from the parts of life that make us say, "I have no idea what I'm doing." But that's not what men are called to do. We're called to take part in God's "family business" of entering into chaos and bringing order.

Since I'm a World War I nerd, I sometimes think about the men who had to "go over the top." After weeks or even months in a filthy, disease-ridden, crowded trench, unable to even look over the parapet, they'd get the orders to go up and into No Man's Land, charging into machine-gun fire. I marvel at their bravery. For me, engaging in real relationships feels like that.

Doing the hard thing, having the hard discussion, saying the thing that needs to be said, is like going over the top. I don't know what's going to happen next.

Sometimes it takes more guts to walk across the street than to travel around the world. Relationships are risky, yes. But withdrawing from them in favor of our comfort is cowardice.

The truth is, I don't think I'm very good at relationships. I'm certainly not a natural. I've always yearned for one very good friend, and if I'm convinced a given person isn't going to be that one very good friend, I don't even want to start a friendship. It's a hassle. It hurts too much. I feel like I let people down.

But I've had to grow in this. I've realized how many other people are lonely. I've also seen that if I can get my mind off myself for a few minutes, I can say a few words and be a genuine difference maker for good in people's lives.

> **Sometimes it takes more guts to walk across the street than to travel around the world.**

Words are powerful. They matter. And people—most people, I've realized—are actually starved for encouragement. It's not just about me getting my needs met. I can think about others. It's worth it, even if I feel dumb sometimes.

Maybe you can relate to that. I don't know. But I do know we're given words for a reason, and God put me in this place, around these particular people, for a reason. Again, no one else is in my exact situation, and no one else is in yours.

Many encouraging, freeing things will simply go unsaid if we don't say them. Being who we need to be takes guts.

The men we need are men with the right ambition: to go into the mess, into the chaos, into the mystery, knowing the Lord is with them . . . and then see what happens.

"That's Awesome, and I Don't Have to Have It"

The Ambition for Contentment

Today I was walking my dog, and I saw an awesome car sitting behind a neighbor's garage. It was a black Porsche Carrera. Unbelievably cool. I've long loved the design of that car. Beautiful.

For a second, I thought, *You know, I could get one of those.* Then I caught myself and reverted to another thought, one that's been extremely helpful in my life. I use it all the time. The thought is countercultural and at the very heart of wisdom in some ways. I'm sure I stole it from someone, so you're welcome to steal it from me.

Here it is: *Wow, that's beautiful! And I don't have to have it.*

I highly recommend this little mental maneuver. And not just for nice cars either. You can apply it to beautiful women who you know are off-limits (possibly because you're already married or she is). *Wow, that's an attractive woman. And I'm not going to pursue her or fantasize about her. I don't need to possess everything that's beautiful.*

Or maybe it's someone else's desirable job or a stunning house in the mountains or a yacht. *Wow, that's amazing. And I don't need it.*

In America, we're taught that we're supposed to seek to possess everything we desire. It helps drive our economy. This is why some will read what I'm writing here and have a negative reaction.

"You're saying it's bad to have a nice boat?"

No, I'm not saying that. I'm saying it's bad to be discontented. Or, better said, it's absolutely fantastic to be content, boat or no boat.

Contentment brings freedom. Discontentment makes you dependent.

Contentment brings freedom. Discontentment makes you dependent. "If I can't have this thing/person/fame/whatever, I won't be satisfied" is a dumb way to live. If you do get that thing, it won't satisfy you for long. If you don't get it—or you lose it—you'll never be happy.

God included this wisdom in the Ten Commandments:

> You shall not covet your neighbor's house. You shall not covet your neighbor's wife, or his male or female servant, his ox or donkey, or anything that belongs to your neighbor. (Exod. 20:17)

God isn't stupid. He didn't include this commandment because he was struggling to come up with a final one to make an even ten. ("I can't just leave it at nine, you guys.") He's telling us this—he's telling *you* this—to let you know some amazingly good news: If you trust him, if you live your life with him as King, you lack nothing. You can go anywhere. You can endure way more than you think. This is key to being ambitious about the right things. There's so much we don't need.

Once, I was part of a team of people trying to help victims of the tsunami in Indonesia. The problem was, after I'd traveled thirty-eight sleepless hours to get to Medan, Indonesia, I found out there wasn't a ticket for me to fly the rest of the way to Banda Aceh. So my team leader put me in the cab of a dump truck headed that way.

It was a thirteen-hour drive overnight.

On a bench seat.

With four other dudes.

Who were smoking.

I sat on the end, squished against the door. I rolled the window down and hung my head out to avoid the cigarette smoke and breathe in the fresh, clean exhaust from the highway.

It might sound like hell on earth. Thirteen more sleepless hours after a brutal series of flights. No real food to eat. No escape from the smoke and the language barrier.

But here's the wild thing: I survived. I put up with it. I handled it. I surprised myself. I didn't even whine that much.

It's freeing to find out you really don't need that much, that you can put up with a lot. Perhaps you've had experiences like that too. Probably not *exactly* like that, though. If you say you had the same five-guys-in-an-Indonesian-dump-truck experience, I will question you.

Anyway, David writes this in his famous Psalm 23: "The LORD is my shepherd, I lack nothing" (v. 1). *Nothing.* I have everything I need to do what I have to do today.

"He makes me lie down in green pastures," David continues (v. 2). As a shepherd himself, he knew that sheep only lie down (quit grazing) in tasty green pastures on one condition: They're full. They can see some beautiful, delicious food a few feet from them but just leave it there.

Contentment is a real thing. And maybe I'll have a Porsche Carrera someday. (It would be highly unlikely but ironically funny. If I do get one, I'll let you know. My next book will be titled *No Way: I Totally Got the Porsche, You Guys.*) Wonderful things are, you know, wonderful. But I don't have to have them. That other radio guy gets a lot of attention? Let him have it. My friend has a pool? Sweet. I'll bring my dog and splash around in it. My neighbor has a beautiful wife? Good for him and her. That guy has better puppet skills than me? Okay, now we have a problem. But the point is, I'm working on it.

I have what I need. The Lord is my shepherd, after all. I lack nothing.

Seriously, try it. One of the most freeing, countercultural things you can say is, "Wow, that's awesome. And I don't have to have it."

Allow Yourself to "Lose"

While ambition is a very good thing, don't confuse it with winning. Many people do.

If I'm ambitious, I must win at my career. I must win the deal. I must win the game. I want to be a winner.

That's ambition, right?

I highly recommend being ambitious about losing. And if I may brag for a moment, I might be the Global Champion of Losing. Some people lose, sure, but I take it to the next level.

I lost a checkers game to a Boy Scout in Kenya. He was surrounded by throngs of friends cheering him on. I got distracted and left myself open (not on purpose) for a game-deciding double-king jump. The crowd went wild and stormed the table. It all got blurry from there, but I think they carried the boy out on their shoulders.

When in Indonesia following the tsunami, our small team of rescue workers camped on the ground near where a group of survivors from a fishing village had taken refuge in tents with their few possessions. One of them had saved his chess set. After they learned to trust us, we had a match for the ages: Muslim Man from Indonesia vs. Strange White Christian Nerd from America. We gambled. I bet my rubber boots that I would win. Again, big crowd. Big pressure. I got smoked. This was not on purpose either. He now owns my boots.

I don't confine my losing to board games either. I'm pretty good at jumping rope, but I lost my first ever jump rope–off to a cocky, pigtailed, "Ooh-aren't-I-great" eight-year-old named Stacey. Again, she had home-field advantage in Ethiopia. I could have done without the crowd chanting, "Sta-cey, Sta-cey . . ."

I started my Global Sports Futility Tour program years ago, when I was hit in the face by a soccer ball traveling at approximately 134 miles per hour. I still remember the Mexican sun framing the silhouette of the six-year-old offender looking down at me as I lay in the dust.

I got a chance to take my baseball skills with me to Kolkata, India, where some middle school kids let me pitch in their sandlot cricket game. I watched their windup style and imitated it exactly. Or maybe I didn't, because everyone was laughing riotously every time I pitched. They couldn't stop laughing. Every pitch of mine was apparently the funniest thing they'd ever seen. I was, and remain, perplexed. I still don't know what I was doing wrong.

I joined a game of soccer on a street in a village in Senegal. It was all adults. It was a friendly pickup game, and they were delighted to have a stranger from America join them. That is, until I repeatedly got smoked on defense, yielding goal after goal. My team soon became icy toward me. The other team smiled at me and made me feel most welcome, which is a testament to their hospitality.

I've even been beaten at Connect Four by kids in the CURE hospital in Zambia. But that was deliberate. I took a dive in those games. No one legit smokes me at Connect Four.

My point? I actually don't mind losing so much. Sometimes losing is just plain winning.

There is a competitive fire in all of us, and it's often a good thing. It can drive us to improve, to stretch ourselves, to make more of what we have.

But we've all seen how the competitive impulse leads us to some very childish places. We don't need more men who simply can't allow themselves to admit that they lost. We don't need more youth coaches throwing fits in front of their kids when a call doesn't go their way. And we certainly don't need more men mentally competing against foes (siblings, high school classmates) for the rest of their lives.

Yes, we're supposed to be all about winning, accept no substitutes, and so on. But it's okay to lose. Really. Losing in style and grace is a sign of maturity, and people admire it. Conversely, have you ever behaved like a petulant child during a game and then won? You may have felt sheepish, and rightfully so. Was it worth it?

You can be driven to excel without losing perspective on what matters. Will Ferrell's Ricky Bobby famously said, "If you ain't first, you're last,"[1] and that line is funny because it's (1) totally dumb, but (2) something that could seriously be on someone's motivational poster somewhere.

Here's a bit of a dirty secret I've learned from knowing some NFL players, and it's something they're not able to say in public. They're not as into winning as you think. (No, I don't have lots of NFL friends, but working in media, I occasionally get to know sports people a bit.) They're not as devastated by defeat as their fans are. You know what they get most excited about? Staying healthy.

You can face defeat with style and grace when you're a secure person. It's that simple. And winners who aren't secure are sooner or later seen as bitter or pathetic.

> You can win at losing. You can do your best, all the while realizing your actual value isn't at stake in the least.

Take it from me. You can win at losing. You can do your best, all the while realizing your actual value isn't at stake in the least.

A friend who is an artist told me about a discussion he had with a professor at his university about value. *How is value determined in the art world? What is something really worth?*

The professor said two things determine value: Who's the creator, and how much is someone knowledgeable willing to pay for the creation?

Think about that with regard to your own value. Take it in. Internalize it.

The right ambition, the best ambition, is to become a man who's so secure, so sure of what his Creator thinks of him, that he knows he's winning even when he's losing.

Don't Be Afraid of Commitments— Be Afraid of *Not* Making Commitments

A final point about priorities and the focus of our ambitions.

We love keeping our options open. But our neighbors and communities need men who *don't* keep their options open.

We need men who commit. That means making choices that cut off other options.

But we live in the time of options. Most humans haven't lived like this, but for us, it's hard to imagine it any other way.

We can't be restricted to just the option of whether or not to, say, have potato chips. We need choices. We need them in big bags and we need them in small bags. We also need them to come stacked in cylinders.

And we won't be stuck with just one kind of cylinder chips either. Just Pringles alone gives us the options of BBQ, Cheddar Cheese, Cheddar & Sour Cream, French Onion Dip, Honey Mustard, and Jalapeño. Or we can have Loaded Baked Potato, Memphis BBQ (not to be confused with non-Memphis BBQ), Pizza,

Salt & Vinegar, Ranch, Sour Cream & Onion, Nacho Cheese, and Southwestern Ranch.

But if we feel limited by this selection, we can also opt for Fiery Sweet BBQ (also not from Memphis), Screamin' Dill Pickle, and Tangy Buffalo Wing. There are the lightly salted, reduced fat, and fat-free options as well. Plus Cheeseburger flavor. And Chili Con Queso. And some more.

There are thirty-four different kinds of Pringles. I counted them.

In America, this is the world we live in. It would be one thing if we had to choose whether or not we wanted some cereal for breakfast, but that's just the start. Walk in the grocery store near you, and there are likely 250 cereal varieties on the shelf to choose from.[1]

Those of us in the modern West are used to being consumers. That means constantly evaluating our ever-expanding options and always looking for upgrades. It's a way of life.

But always keeping our options open is a disastrous way to live when it comes to the things that matter, like relationships.

It's good to decide. Of course, "decide" is a very final word, and a lot of us try to avoid decision making. Decide literally means "to cut off" and comes from the same root word as "incisors" or "scissors."

Commitment means closing certain doors in favor of opening a better one. It means embracing our limits, acknowledging that we can't be everywhere, do everything, or be with everybody at once.

If we don't make decisions, if we don't embrace our limits, we will achieve nothing. It's simple. Want to be a world-class neurosurgeon? You're probably not going to simultaneously dominate on the PGA tour.

Want to have deep, everyday relationships with your neighbors in Portland? You can't live in Oslo.

Want to be an epic father who's remembered fondly for generations for his impact on his friends and family? You can't travel fifty weeks a year for your job.

Want to be a great husband? You can't flirt with other women.

That's how it works. Anything truly poetic we experience in life will be the result of embracing limits. Remaining a free agent forever might seem sexy, but it's a surefire ticket to loneliness. There are things you are free to experience only if you commit, if you cut off other options.

I've been married for thirty-one years. If I had kept my options open, I would not know what it's like to have a woman know me as well as my wife does and still love me. I get to experience the freedom of this kind of love only because I didn't opt for other things or people.

If I had kept all my options open in life, I would not know what it's like to walk my daughter down the aisle like I did a few months ago.

If I had kept all my options open in life, I would not know what it's like to pin a military officer's insignia on my son. I'm so proud of him and who he is (which you've probably picked up on by this point in the book). I've gotten to live alongside this man every single step of the way, from crying infant to combat-medal recipient.

> Remaining a free agent forever might seem sexy, but it's a surefire ticket to loneliness.

I admit I didn't really know what I was doing when I got married. I'm not sure anyone does. It's too profound to fully take in. I didn't know how it would turn out. I didn't know how I'd be pushed to change and grow. I didn't know all the costs and benefits.

But I did know this: I was choosing this woman and cutting off all other options, and much beauty in my life has flowed from that decision.

We don't like being bound to things. We like being open and available to a better option that might present itself. It's human. (Adam and Eve fell for this kind of thinking.) But that's not how real freedom is found. Ironically, we find more freedom when we bind ourselves to the right things—to life-giving things and things that last.

I'm not saying you have to get married to experience the fulfillment that comes with commitment. But it is true that it's not good for a man to be alone, and relationships are sustained by commitment.

I suppose I'll always struggle with regrets about this or that dumb thing I've done. But I promise you that on my deathbed I won't look back and think, *You know, I should've kept all my options open.*

No, I'll remember the look in my daughter's eyes and how pretty she was on a spring day as I walked next to her in the dappled sunshine, and when asked the question, "Who gives this woman to be wed?" I got the chance to say, "Her mother and I do."

Decision Four

Make Women and Children Feel Safe, Not Threatened

How to Treat Women

The Bridger Master Class

We already talked about why we need to be protectors of the gardens God puts us in, but what does that look like, practically?

Sometimes it's the *really* young guys who show us how it's done.

There's an Instagram post that went viral in 2020 of a little boy and a tiny girl. He has his arm around her. They're cute, but that's not what you notice. What you immediately see is that the boy's face is severely lacerated. There's a massive cut from his swollen lip across his cheek all the way up to his swollen left eye. The entire left side of his face is wounded.

His name is Bridger, and he was playing with his four-year-old sister outside their home in Wyoming when a snarling German shepherd set out for her.

And Bridger stepped in.

Why'd he do it? After he got out of the hospital—ninety stitches later!—he told his dad, "I thought if someone should have to die, it should be me."[1]

Bridger gets it. And he's only six years old.

While the incident itself is profound, the reaction to it was too. The story was massive. It was on the national news and all the big network morning shows. It was shared tens of millions of times on social media. Hollywood even got involved: The cast of the *Avengers* movies sent Bridger gifts and connected with him in video calls. Chris "Captain America" Evans sent him his own shield.

When people see men (even six-year-old ones) doing what men are made to do, they sense that it's deeply right.

Bridger is a keeper of the garden. It's obvious his parents have instilled this in him. I hope he keeps this mentality as he grows up, and I suspect he will. If he does, his sister will continue to respect him and feel safe around him. And you can bet his future wife and kids will too.

I'm trying to be this kind of man, a man who makes his wife feel secure and protected. I know my wife is every bit my equal. I know she's highly intelligent and strong and creative and funny. I know she can survive with or without me. But it's my goal to see her thrive and flourish. I believe in her so strongly, I'm excited about what she can yet become.

Currently, she's a tutor and mentor to kids from difficult family situations. She's brilliant at it. I want to add value to what she does, help give her confidence, and be her biggest fan. I don't want to give her things to worry about in my own behavior.

I've learned that Carolyn loves it when I make her feel secure. She loves it when I'm consistently kind and controlled. She loves knowing that I'm not leaving. She loves that I don't flirt with other women. I want to make it obvious to her that of all the possible concerns in her world, she doesn't need to worry about what I'm up to or where I'm going. I'm going nowhere.

I'm convinced that's my job as a husband. Does she wish I could fix cabinets and stuff? Sure, but not much. She's mostly concerned that I care enough about the cabinets to get them fixed if they need it. It matters to her that if something matters to her, it matters to me too. (I just reread that last sentence, and I like it, so I'm keeping it.)

Another thing I've learned: What seem like small things to me are often big things to her, and that's not because she's being illogical. If I leave my socks on the floor, it can seem like a dumb thing to argue about. They're just socks, right? But Carolyn told me something that stuck with me: It's not about the socks. *It's about whether I care.*

That's always the question, even in long-term, successful marriages: *Do you still care? Do I still matter to you?*

This isn't just what weak humans want to know. It's what all humans want to know, even brilliant, strong ones. That's how marriage works, and I chose to get married. Marriage is intense.

> **What seem like small things to me are often big things to her, and that's not because she's being illogical.**

I'm learning—still learning!—about what it means to be a good husband and a good keeper of the garden, and about how to treat the women God gave me.

We want to learn from the best, of course. So I give you another master class . . .

How to Treat Women

The Jesus Master Class

Let's start with a quick look at how Jesus treated women. Since I'm an apprentice of Jesus, I want to learn how he does things and then do them myself. And here's what I'm learning:

1. *Jesus respects women.*

How he went about doing this was shocking in his day. In fact, it's still shocking in many traditional cultures.

There's a story that's familiar to many Bible readers, in which Jesus is visiting a pair of sisters, his friends Mary and Martha:

> As Jesus and his disciples were on their way, he came to a village where a woman named Martha opened her home to him. She had a sister called Mary, who sat at the Lord's feet listening to what he said. But Martha was distracted by all the preparations that had to be made. She came to him and asked, "Lord, don't you care that my sister has left me to do the work by myself? Tell her to help me!"
>
> "Martha, Martha," the Lord answered, "you are worried and upset about many things, but few things are needed—or indeed only one. Mary has chosen what is better, and it will not be taken away from her."
>
> Luke 10:38–42

The takeaway from this story, as I was always taught, is this: Mary is willing to take time out to spend time with Jesus, and Martha is just too busy. Jesus teaches her a lesson about her busyness. That's supposed to be the lesson here.

But that doesn't quite catch it, as it turns out.

I've realized this in my own travels. In some cultures, when I've been in people's homes, I don't see the women. They stay in the kitchen. Only the men are allowed to sit in the living room or dining room on the floor. When food is served, it's slid under a curtain into the room where we men are congregating. Or children are allowed to bring it in.

So catch what Jesus is doing here. He's arrived with his own group of men, and they're talking in another room, likely waiting for the meal to come.

Mary joins them. She sits with them—the men—at the feet of Jesus.

Jesus doesn't send her away. She belongs.

This may seem inconsequential to you, but in the environments I've been in, this would have been strange and, to many, offensive behavior. Mary is doing something radical for that time and place, but Jesus says she's doing the right thing, and he's got her back.

2. Jesus actively listens to women.

There's another famous story in John 4 involving Jesus and a woman with an embarrassing reputation. He encounters her at a well outside the village. John notes that the meeting happens around noon. It's possible that the woman's reputation is so bad and she is such an outcast that she has to go to the well in the middle of the day to avoid being with others.

Jesus talks to her. He listens to her. Intently.

She's taken by surprise. Not only is she a woman, and likely a stigmatized one at that, but she is also a Samaritan. All of these things added up means she fully expects to be ignored.

Jesus' disciples were off getting some lunch, and when they come back, they're "surprised to find him talking with a woman" (John 4:27). At the time, Jesus is likely dealing with all the things that normally lead us to fail and make excuses. He is probably tired, hungry, thirsty, and lonely. But he still honors the woman.

She finds that she has no reason to feel threatened. Not only does he not take advantage of her or diminish her, but he empowers her.

> **The first Christian missionary in history . . . was a woman.**

You can read the whole story, but let me spoil the ending: This woman starts to believe that Jesus may be the Messiah. She runs into her village to tell people about him. They invite Jesus to stay with them, and after he does, many of them become believers.

There have been hundreds of thousands, maybe millions, of missionaries who have gone into communities to tell people about Jesus of Nazareth.

But the first Christian missionary in history . . . was a woman.

3. *Jesus defends women.*

There are various ways he does this, but I want to home in on one particular event, when a woman was caught in the act of adultery and was facing a vicious, humiliating punishment.

Jesus is teaching in the temple courts at dawn, so the religious leaders decide to trap him. Their laws call for the shamed woman to be stoned, but what does he think should happen?

Jesus defends her.

He doesn't do it with a supernatural show of power or muscle, though he certainly could have. He uses his intelligence. He uses his words.

He essentially tells the men, the religiously correct stone holders, "Go right ahead and do it . . . as long as you haven't sinned."

I imagine there's silence and confusion, then the sound of stones dropping. And maybe some muttering as the men scatter. They all leave. The woman is left with Jesus.

> Jesus . . . asked her, "Woman, where are they? Has no one condemned you?"
> "No one, sir," she said.
> "Then neither do I condemn you," Jesus declared. "Go now and leave your life of sin." (John 8:10–11)

Once again Jesus is giving us a brilliant picture of masculinity done right. Where Adam had failed (he let a woman face an enemy without saying a word), Jesus rises to this woman's defense and sends her enemies scurrying away.

Think about this: Our culture specializes in *uncovering* shame—particularly that of women—explicitly and for the disordered delight of others. Uncovering shame diminishes and exposes and dehumanizes.

But Jesus stands up to that culture and *covers* shame.

If you're going to be like him, you'll do the same.

Understand What "Love" Is and Isn't

I think you already understand the basic idea of what real love is. This is so basic I don't need to write it, but here I go: *Real love means wanting the best for someone.*

If you do not desire that for someone, you do not love that someone. It's that simple. You may say you love them. You may think you love them. But no, you don't love them.

Now, to be sure, the word "love" gets used for practically everything. A friend might say to you, "I love this woman I met," and he might mean a hundred different things, but ninety-nine of them aren't about wanting the best for that woman. He might mean, "She attracts me," "She makes me laugh," "She makes me feel good," "She makes me feel important," or "She excites me."

All of this "love" can be roughly distilled into one idea: "I love how I feel." Or, even more briefly: "I love me."

That's it. Most of the time, when we use the word "love" in our culture, we're talking about our love for ourselves. The other person is a means to an end. *I am a consumer, and if she provides me what I'm looking for, I will continue to consume what she can offer. And if she ceases to provide the good self-feelings, well, I must not love her anymore.*

We use the word "love" this same way to describe experiences: "I love going to a Nickelback concert." (That's a throwback inside joke for my fellow old people.) Why? Because we like the feelings we experience when they hit the distortion in "Photograph."

Or we use it to describe authors: "I love J. R. R. Tolkien." (And boy, do I ever.) Why? Because of the entertainment he provides me, the "aha" insights I gain from him, the vicarious adventure, and the sense of togetherness I feel when I read his stories of fellowship or about his friendship with C. S. Lewis.

> **Most of the time, when we use the word "love" in our culture, we're talking about our love for ourselves.**

I even use the word "love" to describe food: "I love pizza." Do I want to see pizza reach its full potential? Will I sacrifice myself to protect it? Am I interested in its long-term good? No. By "love," I mean I want to rip it apart and digest it. By "love," I mean I want to wring every possible good feeling I can draw from its warm, tangy, cheesy, crusty goodness. I want the feelings it can give me. And if it's destroyed in the process, fine. In fact, I'll destroy it *because* I "love" it.

This is the common way women are treated by men, as things to be consumed and experienced. If she doesn't provide the feelings we're after, well, we move on.

This is a betrayal of our God-given role as keeper of the garden. We are doing the work of the enemy. We become destroyers and predators instead of protectors.

The point of real love is to want your loved one to thrive and flourish. It may mean—and in marriage it *will* mean—self-sacrifice. This is the kind of love that redeems and sustains, the kind that sees potential and promise even when the beloved may not see it.

If you have this love toward your wife—the sort that seeks good in her life, the kind that's excited when she continually grows and shares her intelligence and gifts with the world—you will be a fantastic husband. You'll know you love a woman when you want to see her become everything she could be, even if it means your own inconvenience or hardship.

If your "love" for a woman dies when she fails to give you good feelings, you didn't love her; you loved you. But you can choose to love her. Even now, even if you've been married five or twenty years. Love is always a choice.

Richard Selzer was a surgeon and an instructor at Yale and wrote a classic book called *Mortal Lessons: Notes on the Art of Surgery*. In it, he relays a real-life story about love as a choice, and it's been quoted a million times. I'm going to make it a million and one because it's that good:

> I stand by the bed where a young woman lies, her face postoperative, her mouth twisted in palsy, clownish. A tiny twig of the facial nerve, the one to the muscles of her mouth, has been severed. She will be thus from now on. The surgeon had followed with religious fervor the curve of her flesh; I promise you that. Nevertheless, to remove the tumor in her cheek, I had to cut the little nerve.
>
> Her young husband is in the room. He stands on the opposite side of the bed, and together they seem to dwell in the evening lamplight, isolated from me, private. Who are they, I ask myself, he and this wry-mouth I have made, who gaze at and touch each other so generously, greedily? The young woman speaks.
>
> "Will my mouth always be like this?" she asks.
>
> "Yes," I say, "it will. It is because the nerve was cut."
>
> She nods, and is silent. But the young man smiles.
>
> "I like it," he says. "It is kind of cute."
>
> All at once I *know* who he is. I understand, and I lower my gaze. One is not bold in an encounter with a god. Unmindful, he bends to kiss her crooked mouth, and I so close I can see how he twists his own lips to accommodate to hers, to show her that their kiss still works.[1]

A woman is not a product to be consumed. If you're going to use the word "love," if you tell a woman that you love her, remember this: At the very heart of love, real love, is security.

It means "I choose you. I will not stop choosing you."

It means "I will not abandon you."

It means "No matter what, this kiss will always work."

Don't Live with a Woman Unless She's Your Wife

I had a conversation with a caller on my radio show who started with, "I live with my girlfriend and our son. We know we're going to get married someday. So what's the difference, really? It's just a piece of paper."

"Okay, so, honest question," I said. "What's stopping you from getting married?"

"What do you mean?"

"Honestly, what's stopping you from marrying her right now?" I genuinely was curious. "You say you're committed to her. You're giving her your body, and you're taking hers. So why not take a vow in front of her family and friends and yours?"

"Finances, I guess."

"But you live together. What's more expensive about living together as a married couple?"

"I don't know," he said. "I mean, I just want to make sure I can provide for her and my son."

"So you've got a son with her?"

"Yeah. He's two."

"You say you want to provide for him. Why not provide him and his mom with the security of a man who is never going to leave?" I asked. "Why are you writing checks with your body that your soul won't cash?"

"I hadn't thought about it that way. I think you're right."

"Really?"

"Yeah, I think you're right. I think I just didn't want to take responsibility. I need to step up."

"I think you're my new hero. Most of us just justify ourselves. Very few guys will rethink like that. Much respect."

Guess what? A woman wants her man to commit to her. Make no mistake about that. A man's commitment to her, come what may, provides security and reassurance in a chaotic world. She doesn't want him to use her while he keeps his options open. That should go without saying—like much of this book—and yet apparently it has to be said.

Men and women are made in the image of the Creator. Genesis 1:27 says,

> God created mankind in his own image,
> in the image of God he created them;
> male and female he created them.

So sex is an act of re-creation. There's something very mystical and deep happening for both male and female in an act of union. It's a coming together of two facets of God's image.

Jesus actually says this is why marriage exists, to bring together male and female as one:

> "Haven't you read," he replied, "that at the beginning the Creator 'made them male and female,' and said, 'For this reason a man will leave his father and mother and be united to his wife, and the two will become one flesh'? So they are no longer two, but one flesh. Therefore what God has joined together, let no one separate." (Matt. 19:4–6)

So if you're living with a woman without marrying her, you're acting out this mystical "one flesh" with your body but not with your soul. You're valuing keeping your options open more than you are valuing her. You're taking her without fully giving yourself.

You're also acting in a way that will be your undoing. You will disintegrate—literally, dis-integrate. It's the opposite of integrity, a falling apart that happens when the body, soul, and mind are acting out of order with each other.

You may also be contributing to the woman's dis-integration. Your body is proclaiming oneness and protection for her. The rest of you isn't. You're acting out a lie.

Sex in the context of commitment—body, soul, and mind—is creative and secure. Sex out of this context is the opposite. It's destructive, to her and to you. You can "make it work" for a while outwardly, but ultimately acting in dis-integrity corrodes all facets of life.

> **If you're living with a woman without marrying her, you're acting out this mystical "one flesh" with your body but not with your soul.**

I hope if you're cohabitating, you can read this with an open mind. And I hope it's not a guilt trip. I've had to make changes in my own life. That's part of growing into the men God wants us to be. What's more, he's good, and he's quick to forgive us. Life is about humbly learning and changing.

The guy I talked to on the phone called me back the next week. He and his girlfriend had gotten married. Apparently, she was just waiting for him to act. Again, I have a lot of respect for the guy taking responsibility for the woman he loved and the little boy who needed the security of a home with mom and dad forever. That's a very good thing.

Body, soul, mind—all together now. That's integrity.

Protect Them . . . from You

This short chapter is about gentleness, and I can guess the response, because I'd be thinking it: "Let me guess: I should be gentle. Yes. I got it. I can skip this."

But don't skip this chapter. You need to read it because it's probably not exactly what you think. Also, I'm trying hard to write it up real good for you. All this work slaving over a hot computer and you just skip the chapter? No sir.

As I mentioned, I'm not the classic manly guy. As a flute-playing, non-hunting, can't-fix-anything man, I don't have a particularly negative reaction to being told that I need to be gentle.

After all, I've never abused anybody. I've never been a bully. I've never been a guy who hurts vulnerable people. I don't injure people. That's not how I roll.

The only problem is that every sentence I wrote in the previous paragraph is a lie.

I *have*, in fact, abused people. I *have* been a bully. I *have* been a guy who hurts vulnerable people. It *is* how I roll.

Oh yes, I've done it and sometimes continue to do it. I do it with my words.

I'm a master of verbal subtlety. Most people are, I think. Like Dallas Willard has pointed out, we bless or curse people in every interaction with them, and even the slightest pause in a conversation

161

can be a curse. (For example: "Do you love me?" Pause. Slightly longer-than-normal breath. "Sure I do.")

Our coworkers, wives, friends, children, and bosses are often at the mercy of our words and our blessings and curses.

A gentle gardener knows he can easily kill a beautiful, precarious, precious new growth poking out of the soil. But he doesn't do it.

(By the way, I know one popular definition of *gentleman* is "a man who can play the accordion but doesn't." As an accordion player, I reject this.)

To be a gentle man is to be the sort who is more than capable of hurting the weak . . . but doesn't do it. Look at Jesus as the example of living this out. The prophet Isaiah describes the Messiah this way:

> A bruised reed he will not break,
>   and a smoldering wick he will not snuff out.
> In faithfulness he will bring forth justice. (Isa. 42:3)

Jesus calls himself gentle. "I am gentle and humble in heart," he says (Matt. 11:29). Anyone who trusts him will find rest. We can be around him and we won't feel threatened. We can relax. This is how the vulnerable should always feel around us.

As a reminder, we're talking about the King of Kings. He is not lacking in power or the willingness to use it. Here's a description of Jesus in Revelation 1:

> I [John] turned around to see the voice that was speaking to me. And when I turned I saw seven golden lampstands, and among the lampstands was someone like a son of man, dressed in a robe reaching down to his feet and with a golden sash around his chest. The hair on his head was white like wool, as white as snow, and his eyes were like blazing fire. His feet were like bronze glowing in a furnace, and his voice was like the sound of rushing waters. In his

right hand he held seven stars, and coming out of his mouth was a sharp, double-edged sword. His face was like the sun shining in all its brilliance.

When I saw him, I fell at his feet as though dead. Then he placed his right hand on me and said: "Do not be afraid. I am the First and the Last. I am the Living One; I was dead, and now look, I am alive for ever and ever! And I hold the keys of death and Hades." (vv. 12–18)

So Jesus holds the stars, shines like the sun, and holds the keys to death itself, and his eyes are blazing fire. He's also got a sword coming out of his mouth, which I can't quite picture, but it's awesome that he can do that.

All that and he's here to give us rest if we want it. This sounds like a guy to emulate, the ultimate Keeper of the Garden.

Weirdly, we all have "swords" in our mouths, in the sense that we can cut people mercilessly with the words we choose. We can leave them on the floor, bleeding.

It's likely that there are people you could talk to right now, if you so desire, and damage permanently. Your power is scary. Be gentle. Don't betray your role.

Stay silent when needed, but never passive. Actively decide to wield your words carefully. Wield them to always defend and never wound the vulnerable people around you.

This is particularly challenging for me. Not only did I grow up the nerdy sort, but I was also physically small with a neurological disability that practically begged to be made fun of by elementary, middle, or high school guys. To make things worse, my family moved often during my school days, so I repeatedly found myself exposed to entirely new, fresh batches of potential jerks.

My means of defense? My words. I was a quick thinker. My verbal sword became razor sharp. It's how I survived. Want to make fun of the little kid with the shaking head? You can, but know that you will be quickly mocked, spectacularly and publicly, in front of your classmates. People will think you're stupid because Brant will diminish and demolish you with his put-downs.

Words are my thing. Probably yours too. Most of us don't have the problem of routinely hitting people around the workplace. (If this *is* your problem, let me know, and my smash follow-up book will be called *Hey Guys, Stop Routinely Hitting People around the Workplace*.) But we often attack nonetheless.

Be a gentle keeper of your garden. Protect with your words. Build up with your words. Don't betray your role.

In his excellent book *The Masculine Mandate*, Richard D. Phillips shares a revelation from a friend. It has stuck with me, and I hope it sticks with you.

> I used to think that if a man came into my house to attack my wife, I would certainly stand up to him. But then I came to realize that the man who enters my house and assaults my wife every day is me, through my anger, my harsh words, my complaints, and my indifference. As a Christian, I came to realize that the man I needed to kill in order to protect my wife is myself as a sinner.[1]

Yes, we must protect. And it starts with protecting the vulnerable people around us . . . from us.

If/When You Have a Wife and Kids, Remember, They Need You Right *Now*

Speaking of protecting people and things from us . . . I'm trying to learn about plants. Not in an in-depth, horticultural way. More in the "How can I possibly maybe not kill this thing instantly?" kind of way.

There are positive signs. Oh, I'm still killing plants, sure—lots of them. But fewer. The rate of killing has dropped. That's an important first step. ("How's it going, Brant?" "Well, my rate of killing is dropping." "Cool.")

I'm also learning that there are seasons to things. That's less obvious here in Florida, but still, there's a time to plant and a time for things to bloom. There's a time to cut back. There's a time to fertilize and water. Timing is big.

Please consider this in your own life. We're smacked thousands of times a day with marketing messages for awesome products. I don't know that I've ever seen or heard an ad that includes, "This item is cool, but you should probably wait before getting it."

No, the implicit (if not explicit) suggestion is always "NOW!" It's very difficult for us to think in terms of seasons.

Here's where I'm going with this: If you're married with kids, now is the time to be home a lot. It's not the time to relentlessly do "whatever it takes" to build your career. Now is the time to concentrate on the people around you, the ones depending on you.

This is your garden. Keep it. Don't leave it.

You get one shot at this, and it's only for a season. Now is the moment to make financial and lifestyle sacrifices to make time with your family.

I hear the objections: "Yeah, sure, but if I did that, we'd have to rent a place in a trailer park!"

So rent a place in a trailer park.

"I'd have to sell my awesome truck. Are you saying I should drive an old $2,000 Corolla or something?"

Yes. That's exactly what I'm saying. You can drive an awesome truck later. Really. For you, it's not Awesome Truck Season. It's Kids Season. Awesome Truck Season can start later.

Yes, everybody else already has a new truck. But I've had to realize that simply doesn't matter. I *can* drive an old vehicle. I don't *have* to have car payments. An old Ford Focus isn't nice enough for me? I'm too good for a used Hyundai? Who am I, James Bond?

So we can't live in a house where everyone has their own private bathroom? Really, it's okay. Who are we, the royal family of Abu Dhabi?

Let's say your wife has to work a stressful job she hates because of the payment on your oversized house. Are you okay with that? I sure hope you deeply, thoroughly enjoy having that walk-in closet. I pray that oversized garage will bring you great peace.

"Okay, but what about my golf hobby? If I didn't work so much, we couldn't afford it."

Golf later. When you're older. I've heard some people do that.

"We couldn't take any vacations!"

Buy a little inflatable pool, put it outside your trailer, and spray your trailer kids with your trailer hose. It's like a fancy water park without the lines and the $14 turkey legs. They'll love it.

And they'll never forget it, Dad. All that time giggling and playing with you.

"But what about my kids' college fund? Sure, I'm gone a lot and stressed out, but I'm busting my rear end to help them get into a great college."

That's a big mistake. They don't need a college fund. They need *you*.

You're not charged with getting your kids a lucrative career. You are charged with shaping their character. The security they need right now isn't financial security. It's I-know-my-dad-and-he-knows-me security.

If you've got surplus money to put away for college, great. Congrats. But that's a far cry from what some people do: work themselves to the bone and take on extra hours—which stresses out both mom and dad—to make sure their kid gets into this or that school for future career purposes.

And it misses the point. You have them *now*. You're needed *now*. They need you to relax *now* and quit modeling *now* that the point of our existence is career advancement, before they internalize that lie. They need to see you, and lots of you, living a life of contentment in all circumstances. If and when you hit financial tough times, they need to hear you praying through those times.

They'll always remember those moments. They'll tell stories about them.

If your kid becomes a doctor but doesn't truly know you, and she never got to see your real love for your neighbors, well, you missed the point, and you don't get do-overs.

> **If your kid becomes a doctor but doesn't truly know you, and she never got to see your real love for your neighbors, well, you missed the point, and you don't get do-overs.**

You've got them *now*.

Many of us would like more money, more prestige, a more impressive career, but those are not the point of life. And if you believe they aren't, prove it. Act out that belief in front of your kids. After all, what we believe is not what we *say* we believe, it's what we actually *do*.

"But this makes it all sound so simple . . ."

Some things are that simple. You may recall the old saying, "No one ever says on his deathbed, 'I wish I'd spent more time at the office.'" I'm sure that's true. (Unless there was a guy who realized he was on his deathbed and wanted to be ironic: "You know what? I think I'll be that guy who actually says that thing about wishing I'd spent more time at the office.")

Ultimately our lives are entirely about relationships. That becomes crystal clear in the deathbed scenario. It becomes clear in an emergency too. If the house is on fire and family members are inside, we don't run in to rescue the leather couch.

As terrorists crashed planes into buildings on 9/11, I don't know of anyone thinking in the moment, *You know, I think I want me an Audi*. No, what everyone wanted was to call their loved ones, wherever they were.

When confronted with reality, we're very aware that our lives are always about relationships. There are windows for particular relationships that open and then close forever.

Don't buy stupid stuff that interferes with your family life. Don't make financial decisions that wind up stressing out you, your wife, or your kids. It's not worth it.

Too many people can't even fathom having an unhurried family life. They think they simply *must* do this or that job and work these hours, but often it's to support a lifestyle that isn't necessary at all. It's another swindle.

They had one shot. Now it's gone.

Life is short, and it's about relationships, relationships, relationships. That means living at a pace of life we choose, not one that's dictated by our ever-escalating material expectations. Amazing how buying into a "lifestyle" can cost us the lives we really wanted.

If you've got kids in the house, they are your garden to keep, guard, cultivate, and protect. We need men—wives and children need men—who don't forget what their role is.

This is hard and beautiful and challenging and sweet and frustrating and life-giving and breathtaking and . . . it's only for a season.

Do. Not. Miss. It.

More on Being a Husband and Father

Stay at Your Post

If you are single, be content with it. Become a man after God's own heart, one who strives to be a father to the fatherless and a champion of widows and orphans. Even if it's your goal to one day be married, use the time now to grow in wisdom. Enjoy doing what you are given to do today.

If you are married, be content with your wife and your married life. Reconcile yourself to marriage. You chose it. There are things you may miss from the season of your life that was singlehood, but this is a new season, and it's a very good one. Embrace your status as a married man. And embrace your wife. A lot.

If you are a father, own that role too. This isn't the time to take over the world. This isn't the time to maximize all income possibilities. I know I said this before—maybe a couple times—but I really mean it: This dad thing doesn't last forever, and you only get one shot.

You have a garden to keep, and right now it's springtime. Pour yourself into your marriage. Grow those kids. You can't do everything at once. Fall is coming soon enough.

Our culture may tell you you're not being enough when you fully lean into being a dad. It may try to make you think you're not doing enough right now to be significant. It will say you need a more impressive-looking garden to keep, and you need it right now.

Our culture is lying.

I listened to a friend talk about his highly successful career in music. He was traveling the world, playing gigs in front of huge crowds in his rock band. He and his wife had four kids, so he finally made the decision to stop traveling. When he told his wife, she broke into tears. "I could literally see a physical reaction in her, like a weight was lifted off her shoulders," he said.

> **You have a garden to keep, and right now it's springtime. Pour yourself into your marriage. Grow those kids. You can't do everything at once. Fall is coming soon enough.**

He was thankful for the years with the band, but he wondered, What had he put his wife through? Why hadn't he allowed himself to see it?

There's nothing wrong with being a rock star. But there may be something wrong with starting a family and then constantly saying goodbye.

I once read a book about a preacher who had incredible "success" when he spoke to big crowds. He became well-known and traveled the world. His wife was left behind with their daughters.

This preacher started what is now a billion-dollar charity to help poor children (one you've likely heard of). He was always gone from home, but there was no doubt he was an important man in the world. Though his wife begged him to come home, he would recall the deal he'd made with God: If God would take care of his kids at home, he would take care of God's children around the world.

The book I read was a memoir written by his daughter. It was hard to read. She'd been hurt deeply. Her mom had suffered for decades. Her sister, another daughter of this worldwide preacher, ultimately committed suicide.

I remembered the deal the "important man" made with God, and I wondered if maybe God hadn't actually signed on to that deal. Maybe the "deal" was a one-sided justification for the man to continue to do what stroked his ego rather than what God really wanted him to do. Maybe God could have used someone else.

Maybe God gave the man a garden he thought was too small, and he failed to keep it. He abandoned his post.

Perhaps I'm particularly aware of this struggle because it was mine too, when our kids were babies. I wanted freedom and autonomy. I kept trying to do the stuff I was used to doing, even though life had changed at home. It was enormously frustrating.

Frustrating, that is, until I made peace with my role as a husband and dad. I threw myself into it. After that, there was joy.

The garden I was given to keep—a little boy and a baby girl and a woman—was beautiful. My job? Helping them thrive and grow and bloom.

Parenting gets a bad rap in pop culture. Even in conversations when my wife and I first found out we were expecting, I kept hearing about how hard it was going to be, how aggravating the kid would be, how this next season of life was sure to be awful.

Here's how it usually goes down, and I share this from experience.

Your wife is expecting. "This is going to be pretty exciting," you say.

They say, "You just wait."

You just wait, because you won't be getting any sleep once that baby's born. It's all over. It gets harder. It gets worse.

Your baby is fun. You think it's hilarious how he's amused by one particular stuffed dog above all other toys.

They say, "You just wait."

Just wait, because when that kid is toddling around, pulling down the curtains and getting into stuff, you can't look away for a second. It gets harder. It gets worse.

Your toddler is a blast. Everything is new and wonderful to her, from puppies to repeatedly crashing towers of blocks. She laughs all the time and wants you to "Do again!"

They say, "You just wait."

Just wait, because when your kid starts really talking, you'll get tired of that sassy mouth. You'll wish she was still a year old. It gets harder. It gets worse.

Your elementary-age kid is an absolute joy. You can take him swimming, play catch with him, and teach him hilarious end-zone dances to amuse your friends.

They say, "You just wait."

Just wait until he's a teenager, because he'll learn how much he doesn't like you and won't want to have anything to do with you no matter what. He'll eat everything, and you'll get tired of him and want him out of the house as soon as possible. It gets harder. It gets worse.

Your teenager is fascinating. You can't get enough of him. He makes you laugh because, well, you saddled him with your exact sense of humor. You get to play video games with him. He beats you at chess, sometimes twenty times in a row. He fills your home with music, first with a screeching sound that, months later, becomes recognizably melodic, and then with the sweetness of Bach on violin. He mows the lawn—not always happily, but he does it. You catch him listening to your favorite bands in his room. He says things that you never thought about before. He grows taller than you.

They say, "You just wait."

Just wait until he moves away, because your heart will break in two.

And for once, for the very first time ever . . .

They're right.

Decision Five

Choose Today Who You Will Become Tomorrow

Attention Is Everything

Who we become is within our control. It's not a mystery. It's predictable. How?

Who we become is a direct result of what we pay attention to.

You should highlight that. Go ahead, I'll wait here. Don't make me come highlight it for you. (Headline: "Author Convicted of Breaking and Entering in Bizarre Highlighting Case.")

It's really important.

"The life we live out in our moments, hours, days, and years, wells up from a hidden depth," Dallas Willard wrote. "What is in our 'heart' matters more than anything else for who we become and what becomes of us."[1]

We're all emotional beings, and we can't always control our emotions. But what we think about has a tremendous effect on our emotions, and we have a great deal of control over what we think about.

Yes, we live in a culture that pushes all sorts of foolishness and evil at us, constantly pinging our eyes, ears, and brains with banner ads and notifications and billboards and commercials and social media posts and messages. It's a bombardment. But taking responsibility for ourselves starts with us. We have to stand guard over our own minds.

> Set your minds on things above, not on earthly things. . . . Put to death, therefore, whatever belongs to your earthly nature: sexual

immorality, impurity, lust, evil desires and greed, which is idolatry. Because of these, the wrath of God is coming. You used to walk in these ways, in the life you once lived. But now you must also rid yourselves of all such things as these: anger, rage, malice, slander, and filthy language from your lips. (Col. 3:2, 5–8)

Not that long ago, I would see Scriptures like this and think, *Yes, yes, sure . . . but that's not entirely realistic.* But dealing with my impurity, lust, greed, anger, and rage is not unrealistic at all. Those all stem from what I'm consistently putting my mind on.

I used to take groups of high schoolers just over the border into Juarez, Mexico, to help build houses. We'd camp in tents outside the city. It was exhausting, sweltering work. Once, near the end of our trip, I asked some of the guys I'd long had a rapport with, "So . . . have you been struggling with lust this week?"

They had an epiphany right there. Lust had been their number one issue back home, but it wasn't in Mexico. They hadn't struggled much at all, even though it was a co-ed group. They told me they simply hadn't had much time to think about it, and without media or the internet, it wasn't the usual constant battle. They were just too busy.

Their minds were on other things. Their lives were structured differently. They were rarely alone. The work was hard, from early morning to early evening. It was full of laughs and making memories, and they could see the meaning in what they were accomplishing, in helping a poor family have a decent shelter. Their minds were occupied by good things, and even in the short run, that made them different people.

What we pay attention to is everything.

We should note just how the word "pay" fits. Our attention is a limited thing, and we have to manage it like finances. When I'm "paying" attention to something, I'm buying a ticket so my brain can attend.

The phrase "attention is the new currency" is common among

marketing and social media experts. It's imperative to them. Why? Because they know that what we pay attention to absolutely influences our emotions and behavior, and that's everything to marketers.

They also know that if they just repeat a particular advertisement over and over, consumers are more likely to view the product as "high quality"—simply because we keep encountering the ad.[2] At some level we think, *This must be a great product, or they wouldn't keep showing it to me.* The very fact that our

> When I'm "paying" attention to something, I'm buying a ticket so my brain can attend.

attention keeps being drawn to something seems to suggest to us that it's an important and valuable something, even if it's not.

We all have desires, of course. But what we pay attention to has an enormous impact on how those desires get fueled.

Yet as powerful as our desires are, they don't need to define us or control us. They aren't all-powerful, after all. They are not the last word about who we are. That's really good news.

Life is hard enough without us actively going out of our way to throw kerosene on our already burning desires. If I'm addicted to, say, FUNYUNS, maybe using my free time to peruse FUNYUNS commercials on YouTube is not an effective way to address that. If I'm already drinking too much and I know it, maybe putting a poster of a delicious, sweating pint o' Guinness on my wall is a bad idea. If I realize I'm way too angry about current events, why poke the Anger Bear with the stick of "news" and opinions I know will make it worse?

(I totally just used the words "FUNYUNS" and "Anger Bear" in the last paragraph, and I just want to take a moment to bask in that. Thank you.)

You get my point. If I want to shape who I'm becoming, I've got to put my mind on other things, better things, and I actually *can* do that.

I am responsible for what I do with my thoughts. I can take them captive, Scripture says, and break them like an experienced rider can break a wild horse. "We take captive every thought to make it obedient to Christ," Paul wrote in 2 Corinthians 10:5.

Do evil or foolish thoughts, or just plain dumb thoughts, pop into my head? Oh, heck yes, they do. But I can catch on. I can recognize what they are. I can replace those thoughts with better ones. I can get busy doing something else. I don't have to beat myself up for stuff that pops into my head.

When that does happen, I can move on. I *have* to move on, or I will never be the man I need to be, and could have been, for others.

I can't mess this one up. Everyone around me is depending on it. It's the same with you. What you pay attention to will affect the people around you, for good or ill.

If the keeper's heart is lost, the garden is lost too.

Foolishness = Pain

If you want to become the you we need you to be, hang out with people who you know also want to be the people we need them to be. (You should know that when I started that sentence, it made sense in my head, I promise.)

Here's what I really mean. Don't be friends with fools. Pick some non-fools.

"Fool" has specific meanings in the wisdom literature of the Bible. You can read Proverbs yourself, and you should, but I'll give you a quick rundown on what fools do.

They love to vent their anger (29:11).

They actually don't even want wisdom (1:7; 23:9).

They don't learn their lessons. They keep saying and doing the same destructive stuff over and over (26:11).

They hate real knowledge of God (1:22).

They don't even want to understand . . . because they're too busy telling you their opinions (18:2).

They can't handle discipline (15:5).

They're quick-tempered (12:16).

They tend to get in a lot of arguments (18:6–7).

They mock people who take repentance seriously (14:9).

You: Hey Brant, you know you just described Twitter, right?

Me (looking at list again): Wow, you're right. Nice catch. And a great point too, because of what Proverbs 13:20 says:

> Walk with the wise and become wise,
>   for a companion of fools suffers harm.

We cannot exempt ourselves from this truism. There's a common cognitive bias that leads us to think, *I'm not being influenced by this message, but other people are.* It's called the third-person effect. It makes the vast majority of us think advertising works on other people, but not us.

The truth is that, like me, you are very influenced by the company you keep, and that includes intellectual company, for good or ill. If you read a lot of C. S. Lewis, you will begin to think like him. If you spend your time consuming angry political commentary, you'll likely be angrily thinking more about politics.

A companion isn't merely someone you're physically hanging out with. It's someone who has your attention.

So, spend time in venues loaded with wisdom? Get wiser.

Spend lots of time with social media? Get more foolish.

And get hurt too. Here's another proverb, and it's become one of my favorites since I discovered it twenty minutes ago when I was searching the word "fool" in the Bible. Why do I like it so much? Bears.*

> Better to meet a bear robbed of her cubs
>   than a fool bent on folly. (17:12)

So you can hang out with fools if you'd like. But for the record, you'd be better off being personally mauled by an enraged mama bear. You know it's serious business when the Proverbs writer brings up enraged mama bears.

*If I could edit the Bible, I'd include more bears. You're not supposed to edit the Bible, so never mind. But still.

Ask God for wisdom. It's the most important thing you can request, and he promises he'll give it to you. Wisdom will spare you and others around you immense pain. That's the thing about foolishness: It always, always, always brings pain.

As I mentioned, wisdom is knowing what matters. Wisdom is understanding the true value of things.

What's worth more: the thrill of knocking down an entire box of chocolate donuts right now, or your fitness goals?

What's worth more: the fun of staying up until 3:00 a.m. to play a game, or being able to function at work tomorrow?

> **Wisdom is understanding the true value of things.**

What's worth more: the taste of a cigarette, or what your doctor just warned you about your lungs?

Sometimes it's not so obvious, of course. But wisdom always helps. Always.

What's worth more: the rush you get from being "right" in the moment, or protecting the long-term relationship with this person you say you love?

What's worth more: learning your lesson now and suffering a bit of an ego blow, or refusing to be corrected so that you keep making the same mistakes, no matter how costly?

Wisdom is more precious than anything else you can ask for, because life is almost nonstop decisions. Some psychologists estimate we make 35,000 decisions a day.[1] Imagine making those decisions while starting from a skewed view about what really matters in life.

I once saw a car race—I'm not making this up—that was a *blindfold* race. The drivers weren't allowed to see. It was on an oval racetrack near Orlando as part of a night of races, aptly called "Crash-a-Rama." I can provide documentation on demand.

Anyway, each car had a passenger who was supposed to describe to the driver what to do. ("Eddie, turn left NOW!!!") The race was set for ten laps.

> Some psychologists estimate we make 35,000 decisions a day. Imagine making those decisions while starting from a skewed view about what really matters in life.

Now, you might think there's no way this could work, that no one would be stupid enough to wear a blindfold and gun the gas when they heard the starting gun. But you'd be wrong, because they totally did, and lo, the lead cars just plowed into the wall at the first curve, and verily, everybody got hurt, and a helicopter had to be called in to take people to the hospital. I felt vaguely guilty for being there, and I'm pretty sure my IQ just dropped another six points writing about it.

The race lasted exactly a quarter lap.

Living life without wisdom is like . . . that. If I don't have wisdom, I don't know where the heck I'm going. (Maybe it's worse. At least the drivers *knew* they were blindfolded.) The crash is coming. It's just a matter of time.

Ask for wisdom. Why not? And if you really want it, make the wise your companions.

You've possibly heard about the classic experiment by Solomon Asch from the 1950s. He'd ask a small group of people a very simple question using flash cards. When he would ask them individually about the lengths of the lines on the cards, they'd have no problem at all with the little quiz.

But in the small groups, there was a setup: Everyone but one person was in on the experiment. They would deliberately give the wrong answer, out loud, first. When the only "real" subject had to answer the simple question . . . it was no longer simple. In fact, 37 percent would get the answer wrong.

Even more amazing is what happened when another researcher followed up this experiment with a similar one, using functional magnetic resonance imaging machines to study brain activity. He expected to find that the subjects would have to use the part of their brain that helped them in social situations or to resolve conflict. After all, there was an obvious answer, but the other people weren't giving it.

But the subjects didn't use that part of the brain. When the others all said the wrong answer, the subjects simply saw the lines differently. *Their perception of reality changed because of the people around them.* That fast.

Choose the people around you, the people closest to you, wisely. You'll become like them. Their thinking will shape yours. They will help you order—or disorder—your values and desires. They will affect your attitude toward life itself. Do not underestimate this.

They will change who you become.

We need men with wisdom. In fact, we're desperate for them.

Walmart Shopping Cart Attack Guy Never Set Out to Be Walmart Shopping Cart Attack Guy

So, a related question: What kind of man do you want to be in your old age?

(A) A secure, peaceful, strong man who is good-humored and attentive to others, who listens intently, offers insight, and is a source of wisdom and hope.

(B) One of those cranky old guys who smacks you with his shopping cart at Walmart.

There's no "right" answer, even though we're all hoping you don't choose Walmart Shopping Cart Attack Guy. But this really is a Choose Your Own Adventure kind of decision. It's very real. It's not just a thought exercise.

We're always becoming something. I've had to realize that each decision I'm making now is shaping that future old guy. I want to wind up like Gandalf, a man of action who is wise and learned, with a twinkle in my eye and an awesome horse. I plan to also name my awesome horse Shadowfax. I'm going all the way with this.

"Every man over 40 is responsible for his face," Abraham Lincoln is reputed to have said.[1] When I first heard that quote, I thought, *That's actually pretty raw of Abraham Lincoln to say. Not fair.*

But he was onto something. We create ourselves over time. We are becoming something, and that something is more and more pronounced. People don't suddenly become angry, bitter caricatures at age seventy. No, they were working on it a long time ago, step-by-step, decision by decision, attitude by attitude, reaction by reaction.

I used this C. S. Lewis quote in a previous book, but I'm going to use it again because it's great, and also because you can't stop me:

> Hell begins with a grumbling mood, always complaining, always blaming others . . . but you are still distinct from it. You may even criticize it in yourself and wish you could stop it. But there may come a day when you can no longer. Then there will be no you left to criticize the mood or even to enjoy it, but just the grumble itself, going on forever like a machine. It is not a question of God "sending us" to hell. In each of us there is something growing, which will BE hell unless it is nipped in the bud.[2]

Hmm. Hell starts as a "mood." The subtle beginning sounds about right, because no one (except for 70s metal bands) ever says, "I *want* to experience hell. I want to set a course right now and continue on the highway to it." No one deliberately sets out for it. No one (this time including metal bands) ever says, "I want to be a miserable, embittered old person."

But we're all becoming something, and we need to be careful about what that is. We can harbor selfishness and bitterness at nineteen and maybe get away with it while we're still youthful. But over time, it will shape us and misshape us.

> **We can harbor selfishness and bitterness at nineteen and maybe get away with it while we're still youthful. But over time, it will shape us and misshape us.**

Think about it like launching a rocket to the moon. The trajectory may be just one degree off at takeoff, and no onlookers will pick up on it. People applaud and finish their picnics. No big deal, right?

Except the rocket will now miss the moon by 4,100 miles.

Just one degree difference, and with time and distance, it's not even close.

God is very interested in who we are becoming. In fact, that's his central concern with us. We will either be more like him and an oasis of peace and strength for others in a chaotic world, or a distorted, twisted grumble machine.

You may be young or middle-aged or already an older adult, but this is a sure thing: You're not getting any younger. Do not discount the impact of the decisions you are making right now. Not only do we need you now; we're going to need you later to be the man God has in mind.

It doesn't mean you have to become Gandalf. (In fact, please don't, because that's my thing. Do Obi-Wan.) But the world is starved for seasoned, other-centered men who can offer guidance and deep kindness.

How do I know this? *I'm* starved for it. I wish there were more men a generation older than me who weren't collapsed inwardly, unwilling (and frankly, apparently unable) to offer themselves for others.

I could write another book, called *The Old Men We Need Right Now*, but it's likely too late. It's up to the rest of us to become those guys, and we need to start presently.

There are exceptions, of course. There are some older men providing examples of who we want to be, and the examples they give us are striking and beautiful.

I have a wise older friend who has eight children, all grown. Most of them are married with kids. It's a huge group, and they all love coming back home to get together. My friend loves seeing them, of course, but as an introvert, it almost overwhelms him. Even so, it's remarkable to see the photos of everyone gathered around him. It reminds me how a man can be like an oak tree. Solid and enduring and able to shelter so much beautiful life.

Or maybe "foundation" is a better word picture. In construction, so much is dependent on the foundation. Even the most magnificent structure above it will crumble if it fails. But few notice it.

I'm a history nerd who's been to Notre-Dame Cathedral, the Roman Colosseum, and Windsor Castle, and I've never heard any tourists talking about the amazing foundations. I never even thought about their foundations until now, actually, and that's just the point. Men who are honorable serve as foundations for their families and communities, but they may never be fully appreciated.

Are you ready for that? I want to become a guy who can handle that. Maybe we're not there yet, but the exciting thing is who we can become: solid foundations for our family, our friends, our neighborhoods.

Let's do it.

We Don't Need More Needy Guys—We Have Enough of Those

"Line up a hundred men. Watch them closely for a week," psychologist Larry Crabb writes. "Seventy or 80 will be ruled by a passion called neediness. Something inside them needs attention."[1]

My experience in the workplace certainly confirms this. Most guys are chafing to be noticed and affirmed and recognized, and you know what? It's understandable. There's a yearning we all have for significance.

The problem is that unless we get over that, we're never going to reach a point where we're finally able to relax and truly focus on other people. I've known many men who were high achievers, wealthy, or famous and still deeply unsatisfied and needing further admiration. It's ugly.

It's just never, ever enough. We can be pathetic, honestly.

We need you to be the non-needy guy. We need you to be the one who doesn't hunger for constant affirmation or admiration. The only way this is going to happen is if you give up thinking you'll achieve "happiness" the usual way: with status, prestige, significance, money, sex, or an awesome Camaro. (I'm not sure why I picked Camaro there.) Those things do promise happiness, and yes, they totally deliver!

. . . For about an hour.

A single friend of mine bought a fantastic new sports car and brought it by my house. He let me drive it, and I told him, "Man, it must be amazing to drive this to work every day!"

He said, "You'd think so, right? But I got used to it after like a week, then I started thinking, 'Maybe I should've bought something even more expensive?' I don't know."

As you may know, life is like that. It's back to the sucker-punch analogy: We think if we just get that thing, that person, that experience, that whatever, we'll be deeply satisfied. But that never quite works, and the neediness persists.

There's hope for us, though, and it's a permanent sense of well-being that comes from pursuing God. It's called joy.

Joy is something that you can have even when your house is burning down. I'm serious about this. You can have it while grieving. You can have it in the midst of societal turmoil. You can have it in prison.

Shocking but true: You can even be joyful while depressed. (I wrote about this in *Blessed Are the Misfits*, in case you're interested in a fuller explanation.) In the Psalms, David speaks to his own depression repeatedly. "Why, my soul, are you downcast? Why so disturbed within me?" he writes in Psalm 42:11. Then he tells himself what he needs to do to address it: "Put your hope in God, for I will yet praise him, my Savior and my God."

Ironically, and for what it's worth, our very neediness for admiration and respect costs us a lot of admiration and respect. A woman might find you attractive at first, but if you are a needy man, she will lose respect for you.

Some (most?) men just won't be satisfied. They need one more admirer, one more fan, one more like on social media, one more sexual conquest—something that will signal significance. As men age, this becomes more and more grotesque. That's why entire

Instagram accounts are dedicated to high-profile preachers and their bizarre, uber-hip, high-fashion clothes and shoes. People can debate whether it's okay to wear a new pair of $1,500 sneakers each week on stage to talk about Jesus. But the deeper issue is screaming out: Why are these guys (some of whom are in their fifties and sixties) still so . . . *needy*?

Nothing against Dolce & Gabbana, but we don't need Dolce & Gabbana Belt Buckle Preacher Guy. In a subscribe-to-my-YouTube-channel world, we don't need men of God who still need our constant admiration and approval.

But a man who is able to sit and listen, to root for others, to be a voice of affirmation and guidance with no significant payoff in mind? Yeah, that guy is refreshing.

There aren't many of that type. We need more.

We need you to become that guy. And this isn't about taking on a tough, I-don't-need-anybody persona. That's immaturity too, because you're still trying to prove something. The point is to recognize this desperate, yawning gap in our lives, this drive for significance, and find satisfaction for it in our relationship with God instead of in one more promotion or compliment or whatever.

> **Why are these guys (some of whom are in their fifties and sixties) still so . . . *needy*?**

Do you know who you are? You're valued by the Creator of the universe. He values you and loves you so much, he wants to change you. He wants you to become the rare, remarkable man who's life-giving to others.

The Greek philosopher Heraclitus said this about 2,500 years ago, and he nailed it: "No man ever steps in the same river twice, for it's not the same river and he's not the same man."[2]

We're all changing, one way or another. Maybe you're reflective enough to think, *Yeah, I'm constantly needing affirmation and another marker for significance.* Fair enough. The great news is that God specializes in changing people.

That is, when they're humble.

So you can become less needy. It'll happen when you actively turn your attention to God more often, spend time praying and communicating with him, and ask him to grow your desire for him. Joy is a fruit of the Spirit. It's something that comes from changing the inputs in our lives, altering our schedules, reshaping our habits, and putting our minds repeatedly on the right things.

You can be the guy who's a source of significance and blessing for others. You'll still struggle with yourself, but you'll become more and more like Jesus. The enemy tempted him with everything the world had to offer. Power! Significance! Prestige!

And Jesus said no.

He didn't need it. He knew who he was.

I hope you do too.

Become a Man without Fear (Seriously)

Fear can stop you from becoming the man you want to be. But you know what? You actually have nothing to fear.

Nothing.

This sounds preposterous to most people. It seems obviously wrong. In fact, most people are driven by fear. They're shaped by it.

I'm sure this also sounded preposterous when Jesus told his followers they didn't need to worry or be anxious about *anything*. How could he possibly say that?

Fear, after all, is the most basic human feeling.

"Ah, but it isn't for me," you may say.

"Yes it is. Think about it," I'll say. "The first thing you ever did was cry."

Stunned by the truth of my retort, you grudgingly acknowledge that I totally just won the conversation.

And it's true—everyone comes into the world crying and screaming. It's like we're all born with a bucket list, and it's not a long one. Here it is:

BUCKET LIST

1. Freak out.

Fear and anxiety are totally human. Totally normal. Totally expected. So was Jesus crazy when he said not to fear? Or was he joking? His audience at the time had to wonder. They were occupied by the Romans. They faced injustice. There was rampant racism. Many people faced food insecurity. And here's Jesus saying don't be anxious about those things.

Maybe you've heard this story in Mark 4:35–41: Jesus is out on a boat with his disciples. A storm kicks up, and it's apparently bad enough that even the experienced fishermen among them are freaking out, thinking they're going to die. Jesus is in the back of the boat, "sleeping on a cushion" (v. 38). (It's odd to me that Mark writes his book with very few details—but he specifically lets us know that Jesus wasn't just asleep, he had a cushion. I just checked, and this is the only time the word "cushion" comes up in the entire Bible. #funfact)

Jesus' friends are panicked, naturally, and they wake him up. "Don't you care if we drown?" they ask, no doubt annoyed and amazed that he can somehow sleep during all of this.

He speaks. The water is immediately calm. He tells his friends he's disappointed in them. Why were they so afraid? It's like they'd learned nothing. They actually had nothing to fear, but they still didn't get it.

They failed the test. And it was a test, by the way. After all, the boat trip across the lake was Jesus' idea. He knew the storm was coming, and he knew he'd be asleep.

They didn't need to be afraid of the storm. And not just because Jesus was in the boat. Even if the boat had sunk, they'd be okay. Even if they had drowned, God had control of the situation. No matter what.

Jesus really *was* saying they had nothing to fear. The entire Bible is very consistent about this. If God is for us, who can be against us? Paul writes that living is great, but dying is a win too. "To live is Christ and to die is gain," he writes in Philippians 1:21.

If I fear God, I need fear nothing else.

Paul writes this to people who thought they might be killed soon because of their faith:

> Can anything ever separate us from Christ's love? Does it mean he no longer loves us if we have trouble or calamity, or are persecuted, or hungry, or destitute, or in danger, or threatened with death? . . . No, despite all these things, overwhelming victory is ours through Christ, who loved us.
>
> And I am convinced that nothing can ever separate us from God's love. Neither death nor life, neither angels nor demons, neither our fears for today nor our worries about tomorrow—not even the powers of hell can separate us from God's love. No power in the sky above or in the earth below—indeed, nothing in all creation will ever be able to separate us from the love of God that is revealed in Christ Jesus our Lord. (Rom. 8:35, 37–39 NLT)

So, seriously, what can others do to you? If I may quote the words of 90s rock band P.O.D., "Is that all you got? I'll take your best shot."

Here's another throwback reference: the 2005 NCAA tournament. I'm a University of Illinois alum, and I remember watching the game live with my kids when they were little. It was a battle for the Final Four. I was nervous.

Illinois struggled. With four minutes left, they were behind by fifteen. It was obviously over. I was bitterly disappointed and told my son we might as well shut it off, what's the point, and so forth. I was acting like a baby.

My little boy didn't want to shut it off. And Illinois staged an epic comeback and won.

Since then, I watch a replay of the game on YouTube every few years. It's still entertaining, and there's still some tension, but it's a totally different experience. I don't get bitter and negative watching it. I don't roll my eyes like I did the first time and say out loud, "This game is over. Forget it. Forget everything."

Why? Because I know how it ends. If I know how something ends, and that it ends well, I have a totally different experience watching it or living it. There's no reason to be anxious. The ref makes a terrible call? That's frustrating, but not really, because I know how it ends.

And Jesus' words assure us that *he knows how it ends.*

Death is the ultimate weapon of our spiritual enemy, but two thousand years ago, it was disarmed.

God is ultimately going to take care of us. Plus, he said, worries don't help, so what's the point? Worrying about tomorrow just makes today miserable.

> Can all your worries add a single moment to your life? And if worry can't accomplish a little thing like that, what's the use of worrying over bigger things?
>
> Look at the lilies and how they grow. They don't work or make their clothing, yet Solomon in all his glory was not dressed as beautifully as they are. And if God cares so wonderfully for flowers that are here today and thrown into the fire tomorrow, he will certainly care for you. Why do you have so little faith?
>
> And don't be concerned about what to eat and what to drink. Don't worry about such things. These things dominate the thoughts of unbelievers all over the world, but your Father already knows your needs. Seek the Kingdom of God above all else, and he will give you everything you need.
>
> So don't be afraid, little flock. For it gives your Father great happiness to give you the Kingdom. (Luke 12:25–32 NLT)

Imagine actually living this way. Who does that? I mean, besides Tony Stark. I remember watching an *Iron Man* movie (I forget which one) and especially enjoying Stark's fun-loving quips when it looked like he was going to die. It's like he knew he'd be fine. It's total fiction, of course, but I honestly believe we could be like that.

People are drawn to this sort of attitude. In a world of insecurity and threats, a secure man who helps others feel secure is very compelling. A keeper of the garden is a man who knows how it all ends, that nothing can separate us from the love of God.

While everyone else is beset with anxiety, it's incredibly encouraging to see someone who takes Jesus seriously and really believes, "The world is a perfectly safe place for me to be. I know how it ends."

No matter what.

What's that? You say you can take my life?

No. You can't.

I already gave it away.

Don't Follow Your Heart—Open Your Eyes

Make no mistake, you are free.

You are created in the image of God, and part of that image is being truly free.

You are free to be your own god if you like. Free to waste your life or do something profound and heroic with it. Free to seek wisdom or be irresponsible. Free to commit your heart, mind, soul, and strength to your Creator or to yourself. Free to flourish or to destroy your own life. Free to say, "God, you are my King," or to say, "I am the captain of my soul" and walk away from God's authority.

You are free to be proud and, in the process, proudly destroy your own life. You are free to deeply harm people who love you. You are wildly free.

It's shocking just how much freedom God allows. If you read the Gospels, you'll see Jesus allowing people to walk away from him all the time.

One example: A rich young man approaches Jesus with a question, wanting to know how to be saved. Jesus knows that this man idolizes his money, so he tells him he needs to sell what he has and give it to the poor.

The young man walks away, sad.

If you're familiar with the idea that Jesus is all about love—and he is, of course—you might expect him to say to the young man, "Hey, wait, let me try to explain it this way to you," or to run up behind him and ask to talk some more.

Surely Jesus loves him too much to just let him walk away, right?

But Jesus lets him go.

There's the prodigal son story too, which you might be familiar with. A young man wants his dad's wealth right now, while he can party with it, instead of waiting until his dad dies. His dad grants him his inheritance, and the son takes the money and goes on a destructive spiral.

One wild thing about this story: When the prodigal son lays out his ridiculous, destructive plan, his dad doesn't say anything. Not a thing. He knows his son is on a path to pain and misery, but he gives him exactly what he's asking for. He doesn't try to find his son and talk him into coming back. He doesn't even send messengers to do it. There is no emergency, maybe-we-can-talk-some-sense-into-him mission.

> **One wild thing about this story: When the prodigal son lays out his ridiculous, destructive plan, his dad doesn't say anything.**

When the son does come back, it's because he freely chose to. At that point, and not a minute before, his father sees him and comes running to meet him.

Part of God's love for you is his commitment to your freedom. It's clear throughout Scripture that he wants very much to enjoy you and for you to enjoy him. But that's up to you.

Of course, freedom is scary because it means that not only are we capable of choosing to do immense good, of bringing immense healing, but we're also capable of causing immense damage.

> The wise woman builds her house,
>   but with her own hands the foolish one tears hers
>   down. (Prov. 14:1)

Think about that. With her own hands, a woman either builds or destroys her own home. She's free to do either one.

And what will be the internal monologue if she's destroying her house? I promise it won't be, *Why, I'm a fool! I'm tearing my own house down! I'm an idiot! Why am I doing this?*

No, that's not how we humans operate. Instead, it'll be, *I'm doing the right thing. You see, it all makes sense because . . .*

We can justify anything. Be aware of this. It's the old trope to "follow your heart." In my last book, I called that "the worst advice ever."

Following your heart is stupid. It leads to destruction. It's the last thing you should do in any matter of importance. Let's say you're married, but you meet an attractive woman who makes you feel great about yourself. You can follow your heart, sure . . . if you want to betray your vow, crush the woman who trusted you, and ultimately destroy everything you have.

Once when I came home, my wife had just gotten off the phone. She was shaken. "Jack is leaving Sarah," she said. (I'm not using their real names here.) "He was calling for you. He said he's willing to talk to you about it, but he's already made up his mind."

I did not see that coming. We'd known them for years. They were both brilliant, accomplished, and hilarious. We spent a lot of time together. Jack and I went to baseball games together. They'd just had their first kid, a one-year-old named Drew. Jack was smitten with his little boy.

I went over to their house, feeling very awkward and unsure of what to do. Jack and I sat at his dining room table, and he explained to me that he was completely in love with a woman from work. They were true soul mates, he said. He actually felt like he was cheating on her by staying in his marriage with Sarah.

He said he knew that he was doing something technically wrong, but his new love was so real, so vivid. It was obvious the two of them should be together and he should leave his wife and son.

The first hour of our conversation, as I recall, was mostly me saying, "What? Seriously?" I couldn't believe this was happening. "Really? I just . . . What the . . . ?" I had no idea what to say.

But then I remembered the breakup of my own parents, and I started going down a list for Jack. It was the "Here's What's Going to Happen to You Now" list, based on my own family experience as well as my observations of others:

> You're going to spend Drew's entire life as something of an outsider.
>
> You're never going to get to coach his baseball team.
>
> Every interaction with him will become a logistical issue instead of being natural, day-to-day life.
>
> Christmases will be a struggle instead of pure joy.
>
> You're going to sit in the back row at his graduation.
>
> You're going to be in an awkward place at his wedding, possibly alongside a longtime stepfather who's been his up-close dad most of his life.
>
> You will look back with regret at crushing a woman who only supported and loved you.
>
> You will absolutely encounter problems with this new "soul mate" and deal with another possible breakup.
>
> You could have been an intimate, wonderfully respected, beloved grandfather to Drew's kids, but instead, you'll be fighting for time with them, if you get any at all.

This was a much longer list, to be sure. But that's what I remember talking about. We walked through the ramifications of what Jack was doing.

Remarkably, he stayed with Sarah. It's even more amazing that Sarah stayed with him. In retrospect, I think the ramifications list was a really good idea. I felt like I actually said the right thing. (Thank you, Lord.)

And Drew's dad coached his baseball team.

When we're hit with a temptation that could destroy everything, we rarely think, *This will destroy everything. It will cost me dearly, possibly for the rest of my life. I will live with regret about the ongoing devastation I've caused. But I'm going to do it.*

No, we usually narrow our focus to avoid thinking about what we're really doing, which is misusing our freedom to hurt and destroy all that we've worked for and all those around us.

Remember this and prosper: Don't follow your heart—open your eyes.

Decision Six

Take Responsibility for Your Own Spiritual Life

What God Is Looking For

Loyalty

This chapter is incredibly important. It could be its own book. Maybe you'll write it someday. I'd buy it.

Growing up in American church culture, I could never quite articulate this question, but I was always wrestling with it: *What in the world does God actually want from me?*

It was confusing because the answer seemed like a long, strange list. I mean, I was pretty sure he wanted me to evangelize, to share the good news. So that was it. That was what he wanted.

But I was also pretty sure he really wanted me to read the Bible. So those two things—evangelism and Bible reading—were what I needed to concentrate on.

Wait. Prayer. That's important. So really, three things.

Also, giving to the poor and that sort of thing. Maybe I could combine that with being an activist for the right causes. So four things, really.

But also serving at a church as a volunteer in some capacity. And giving money to the church. So there's a couple more. Plus joining a small group. Community is important. And singing worship songs with people and listening to sermons are both big. So those two things are vital too—don't forget those. Plus getting baptized. And receiving communion. And also attending Sunday school. And extra services for Easter.

I think we're at around thirteen things so far. So just concentrate on the 13 Big Things, and—

Wait, there's fasting. I think we're supposed to go without food. God wants that. So just concentrate on the 14 Big Things. Also, confessing sin.

So, yeah. The 15 Big Things.

Plus help out at a soup kitchen.

———

To my great relief, I have realized over time that God really wants one thing from us, and here it is, so gird yourself:

Loyalty.

A believing, trusting loyalty. And it's loyalty to him specifically. Loyalty through everything. No matter what.

Now, I'm not especially emotional about my relationship with God. I've heard a relationship with God described simply as a trusting response to a known love. I am loyal to him because he has proven himself to me. What else would he need to do?

I'm also loyal to him because *who else am I going to be loyal to?* Is there a better option? Do you have a better idea? Everyone has an ultimate loyalty. Maybe it's to another god or a political agenda or a career or patriotism or family. But who or what has done more for me? Who or what remains unshakable when everything else changes or collapses?

I'm also loyal to him because he allows me to be. I'm a sinner and an addict. And so are you. We're all addicted to ourselves. I justify and rationalize, and I'm biased toward myself in every interaction. I think about myself nearly every minute of every day. I need help.

And God allows me back! Somehow, again and again.

I'm thankful for Scriptures like the Psalms precisely because I can see what a genuine, honest relationship with God looks like.

Many of the Psalms are attributed to David, who failed God spectacularly in spite of everything God had done for him. David's sin had real-world effects that were devastating and humiliating. But his passionate interactions with God and his steadfast, believing loyalty continued.

Another great example of a man with serious issues remaining loyal is Job. He says many dumb things, and God verbally blasts him for it, putting him in his place . . . right before he rewards Job many times over. Why? Simple: Job remained faithful. He just kept interacting. He failed in many ways, sure, but he never stopped seeking God. He was loyal.

So you're a sinner? Yes. So am I. But we can't let our guilt push us away from God instead of toward him. We have to keep interacting in spite of ourselves. Real, raw prayer—the kind where you're thinking about what you're saying—forces honesty. If your mind is engaged and you're not just defaulting to crutch phrases, you won't be trying to fool God. You'll know you can't. That's one reason passionate, engaged prayer is so healthy.

> **Sometimes you might "feel" God around, sometimes you won't. But that's never the point.**

When it comes to your relationship with God, loyalty is where it's at. Do not define your relationship with God in emotional terms. Sometimes you might "feel" God around, sometimes you won't. But that's never the point. The point is always his enduring loyalty to his people and our enduring loyalty to him.

Loyalty doesn't get talked about much in church circles, but it should. The word that captures this steadfast loyalty best in Hebrew is *hesed*, and it's used a decidedly unsubtle 246 times in the Old Testament. Most of the time, it's used to describe God's loyalty to his people. But it's also used to directly tell us what God wants from us, like he does in Micah 6:8. We're to act justly, love *hesed*, and walk humbly with God.

And not just any God. The God of the Bible is a particular one. In the biblical story, there are many other spiritual beings who are in full rebellion against the Creator. Other nations follow these lesser spiritual beings, ones bent on humanity's destruction, and God continually warns his people not to have anything to do with them. To stay loyal. Over and over, he demands their loyalty and grieves through the prophets when his people turn away. The God of the Bible is a jealous one.

Yes, he loves everyone. But not everyone is bound to him. Not everyone has made a covenant with him. Not everyone has said, "I'm in, I'm your disciple, and you are my authority." Not everyone wants to be loyal to him. They're loyal to something or someone else.

Loyalty means not letting our sinfulness keep us from God. Focusing on our sin can push us away. Trust me, he is not shocked by our sin. He paid a steep price because of it. He knows we're sinners. But as we continue to focus on living a loyal life, turning our attention repeatedly to him and interacting with him, we will change and grow. I've seen it happen in my own life.

If we abandon turning our minds to God and give up honestly relating with him, we won't grow up. We won't become the keepers of the garden that we are meant to be. We'll be hyper-fixated on our guilt, or we'll hand ourselves over to our desires. And they will cripple us.

Of course, no chapter on loyalty is complete without a *Lord of the Rings* reference. Merry had to assure Frodo that yes, his friends were afraid too, but they weren't leaving him. No matter what happened. Ever.

> You can trust us to stick to you through thick and thin—to the bitter end. And you can trust us to keep any secret of yours—closer than you keep it yourself. But you cannot trust us to let you face trouble alone, and go off without a word. We are your friends, Frodo. Anyway: there it is. We know most of what Gandalf has

told you. We know a good deal about the Ring. We are horribly afraid—but we are coming with you; or following you like hounds.[1]

God isn't looking for a scrubbed-up life. If that was his main goal for you, he could force it. He wants way more than that. He's looking for the real you to be loyal to the real him.

That's when the adventure begins.

Angry Men Aren't Attractive to Women, but Men of Action Are

Since I already wrote a book about anger, I thought I'd take the opportunity to interview myself with the usual questions that come my way.

Q: You wrote a book about anger called *Unoffendable*. Did you expect it to tick people off?

A: It wasn't my goal to do that, but I did expect it. We humans *like* being angry much of the time. It gives us a self-righteous rush. Plus there's often real hurt that causes the anger in the first place, and it's so very difficult to say, "I'm forgiving this person, even though they don't deserve it."

Q: Why should someone forgive someone who isn't sorry? Not everyone will apologize, you know.

A: I use "should" because I'm addressing my argument to followers of Jesus, and I'm saying we have to forgive people whether they deserve it or not. After all, God forgives us, and we don't deserve it, do we?

So the basis for forgiveness is simple: We forgive others because that's what God is willing to do for us. And if we

don't forgive others, he won't forgive us. Jesus said that
(Matt. 6:14-15). It's really a remarkable teaching.

Q: But can't we stay angry and forgive at the same time?

A: I'm not sure how that's possible. "I forgive you, but I'm
still mad at you" is . . . dubious. And kind of awkward.
The process of letting go of anger is the very essence of
forgiveness.

Q: But the Bible does say that some of our anger is good,
right? We should hold on to *some* of it, right?

A: No, the Bible doesn't say that. In fact, James 1:20 says,
"Human anger does not produce the righteousness that
God desires."

Q: Okay, but does that mean we have to stay in relationships
with hurtful people?

A: Absolutely not. You can and should let go of your anger
in light of the fact that God has forgiven you. It's a work
of the heart, and it keeps anger from destroying you. But
forgiveness doesn't mean you have to stay in a relationship
with a hurtful person. What's more, I'd say that if you
don't forgive someone, you will stay in a relationship with
them in your head. Forever.

Q: What about when people have "righteous anger"? Doesn't
the Bible talk about that?

A: No, it doesn't. It never affirms human righteous anger. It
does talk about *God's* anger being righteous. He's sinless.
He's entitled to vengeance, and we're not. He is the ultimate judge, and we're not. There are some things that he
can be trusted with that we can't.

Q: Isn't anger kind of masculine, though? What kind of man
doesn't get angry?

A: No, it's not masculine. Toddlers get angry. Anger is hardly
a sign of strength.

It's funny, when I've done interviews about this subject on talk radio, it's usually with a male host who starts flexing about how angry he is about such-and-such issue. He says something like, "I'll be [darned] if I'm going to stand by and allow that to happen! How could you tell me not to be angry about it?"

Anger doesn't change anything. *Action* changes things.

But anger doesn't change anything. *Action* changes things.

Do not confuse the two, as many often do. In my view, it's amazing how little all the "righteously angry" people actually do. They get worked up, maybe fire off some social media posts, and pat themselves on the back for being so righteous in their anger. In fact, they'll get mad if you're not mad enough about the thing they're mad about.

Q: But we need anger to fight against injustice. If I'm not angry, I won't act.

A: That's what the larger culture thinks, sure. But it's not true. Not unless our "fight against injustice" is really just about us, our tempers, our biases, and our unresolved issues.

We ask police, for example, to do their jobs without anger. And we ask judges to do their jobs without anger. Anger clouds judgment and surrenders to bias, and we don't need more of that in our justice system. We ask these people to do their duty because it's the right thing. We don't ask them to get angry.

Our son recently returned from serving in Afghanistan, and I'm proud of the work he did there. He was charged with protecting innocent people from works of evil. I don't believe he did that out of anger. He didn't want anger to cloud his judgment. He just took action, and people are better off for it.

Q: Doesn't anger help sometimes? I mean, what if some-one was trying to attack your kid? Shouldn't you be angry?

A: Yes—in the moment. The fight-or-flight response in a moment of genuine threat that calls for physical feats makes total sense. That's what that system is for. It's part of being human. But it's not to stay with us. Paul writes in Ephesians 4:26 that yes, we'll get angry, but we have to drop that anger the very same day.

A smart friend of mine objects to this and says, "What if there's someone still out there planning to attack your kid? Shouldn't you stay angry to guard your family as long as that person is out there?"

Think about that. To summon the energy to protect my family, I'd need to be angry?

I'd rather be clear-minded. I promise I would be plenty motivated to protect my family without needing to harbor anger.

Q: Still, isn't the Incredible Hulk kind of cool? He gets a lot of stuff done when he's angry.

A: He totally is cool, and he does get a lot done. (Plus he's ripped, and it would be awesome if I could flex just once and my clothes would be in tatters. Just once. I keep buy-ing tighter shirts.) That said, no real woman wants to be married to the Hulk. Women don't want to be around angry guys. They want to be around clearheaded men who manage to get things done without the rage.

Angry guys aren't attractive. Men of action are.

Don't believe me? Go ask some women.

Q: But I'm scared to talk to women. You should write a book that helps us talk to the ladies.

A: Let me remind you that I play accordion. You don't want me writing that book.

Q: So why is this bit about anger in the "Take Responsibility for Your Own Spiritual Life" section?

A: Simple. This is a massive spiritual issue for people. Because we've made anger into a "righteous" thing, we're not taught how cancerous it is to the rest of our lives. As I've detailed in this book, holding on to anger has extensive (and deadly) physical consequences. It torpedoes our relationships.

   Anger is not a fruit of the Spirit. It's a roadblock to experiencing peace, contentment, and joy. It subverts our efforts to grow in other areas. It keeps us from being other-centered.

   Anger stops us from growing up, and boy, for the sake of the world around us, do we ever need some grown-ups.

Don't Confuse Your Emotions—or Lack of Emotions—with Spirituality

Good news about this whole spiritual life thing that bears more discussion: Being "spiritual" simply does not mean being emotional. If you don't get emotional about God or spiritual topics or worship music, it doesn't mean something is wrong with you.

Jesus talks very little about emotions. He talks a lot about something else: obedience.

Obedience is what he expected from the guys he handpicked to be his disciples. (They're called "disciples"—meaning people who pursue the disciplines—not mere believers or admirers.)

Our culture, in and out of church settings, tends to be very feelings-driven. We allow our feelings to determine reality. Jesus, however, is not feelings-driven.

If you do get emotional while worshiping God with others or by yourself, that's fine. But don't confuse emotions with loyalty and obedience to the Master.

(I wrote extensively about this in another book, *Blessed Are the Misfits: Great News for Believers Who Are Introverts, Spiritual Strugglers, or Just Feel Like They're Missing Something*, and I recommend you buy a copy of that book. Maybe seven of them, actually. No, thousands of copies. Build a fort with them. Thank you.)

Just because you don't "feel" God around doesn't mean he has left you. Our feelings come and go based on many things, like whether we are eating well, are dehydrated, or need a nap.

It's apparent from Scripture that God is very pleased when we obey, whether we're feeling it or not. And let's face it, so much of obedience is about acting in a manner directly *opposed* to our feelings. Who *feels* like praying for the people who are persecuting them? Who *feels* like blessing people who curse them? Who *feels* like turning the other cheek and letting some selfish, attacking fool dictate their next move?

Answer: Exactly nobody. Nobody feels that way. Just like nobody feels like picking up their cross daily and living a life of radical forgiveness for the very people who don't deserve it.

We don't feel like it, but we do it anyway. This is the stuff of mature manhood. It's also the stuff of relating to God in a proper way.

There's another word for this dogged obedience: love. This is what love looks like.

You already know intuitively that if you do something because there's a payoff for you, it's not love for anything but self. But if you do it in spite of yourself . . . now we're talking love.

"If you love me," Jesus said, "keep my commands" (John 14:15). If I love God, I will do the things he wants me to do, even without the promise of an emotional payoff. The emotions, frankly, have absolutely nothing to do with my actions.

I think those of us not given to religious emotion can actually live this out more readily than those who associate God with feelings. If their feelings are gone, where did God go? What's left?

If you're not particularly emotional about your faith, don't worry about it. That simply isn't the point. It does not diminish your faith. You have much to offer.

If you get married, your spiritual life may not look like your wife's. She may be more emotive or less. She may wish your spiritual life looked more like hers, or vice versa. Don't get hung up on this. You are responsible for your own pursuit of God, your own willingness to obey.

The issue, as always, is making it your intention to continue submitting to God, turning your attention to him, whether you feel it or not. As James writes, "Do not merely listen to the word, and so deceive yourselves. Do what it says" (1:22).

I met a guy who was a great example of this. Kevin was attending the same church we were, but church was befuddling to him. I could see it.

He was a husband and dad of three kids. He was a man's man. He worked at a factory. He hunted. He drove a motorcycle. Unlike me, he could fix things. He wasn't musical. His wife was, though, as well as artistic, expressive, verbal, and emotive.

He was quiet. His wife was frustrated at his lack of "connection" to God.

I got to know Kevin because I needed him. I was helping out with the high school kids in the church and had planned a trip to Mexico to build a house. Lots of kids wanted to go, but there was one main problem: me. And my lack of ability to plan stuff or build stuff or even work the tool . . . things.

I asked Kevin to go, explaining my situation. He didn't react emotionally or excitedly. I think he was kind of suspicious of a guy from church with no guy skills, whom he barely knew, begging him to do something so out of the usual for him. But I needed his skills big-time.

Kevin said yes, and he was amazing. Irreplaceable. There's no way we would have finished the house without him. He was a workhorse, using his knowledge, muscle, and determination to do what I—or a team of a hundred other flute-playing writers—couldn't.

He was an encouragement to the students with us. He set the tone at the work site and helped people learn new skills. He was a total superstar. The family receiving the house was overjoyed, and Kevin got to see the couple and their little girls move in. They wouldn't have had this shelter without his work.

He told me it was the best couple weeks of his life, and he finally saw that he had a place, a role in the kingdom. Apparently "worship" to him had been defined as attending a stage presentation or a loud worship-themed weekly concert. He didn't resonate with that. But this! This he understood. It was his spiritual act of worship.

So, sure, Kevin is not emotive. He doesn't cry during the worship music. He just said yes and did his thing, and now a family he didn't even know has a home.

We may have made "religion" a primarily emotional experience. But notice how James describes the religion that God actually wants: "Religion that God our Father accepts as pure and faultless is this: to look after orphans and widows in their distress and to keep oneself from being polluted by the world" (1:27).

Spirituality isn't measured in goose bumps.

You Know Enough to Act

I exchanged emails with my high school English teacher not long ago. I apologized to her and told her, "You know that time you said, 'Don't you just love LEARNING things? Just for the sake of learning?' And we students said, collectively, 'Uh . . . what?' Well, *I get it now*. A bit late, but I get it. I love learning now."

A little late, but there you go. I wish I could take her class again.

Knowledge is wonderful. All truth is God's truth, which means we should pursue truth relentlessly in any field we like. Anti-intellectuals will bristle to find out that Solomon himself didn't just ask for wisdom. He asked for knowledge too (2 Chron. 1:10).

So, yes, I'm pro-knowledge. I'm a fan of lifelong learning. I need you to know that before I ask this.

Is it possible you already know enough to do what you need to do?

My friend Sy died recently. He was probably the most brilliant teacher and orator I've ever heard, and he was invited all over the globe to speak to huge audiences. And yet he said that most American Christians, most first-world Christians, most well-educated Christians with bookstores and Bible colleges and resources available, do not need more knowledge. "If you never, ever heard another sermon," Sy said, "and God took you and squeezed you out information-wise all over the deserts of the world, you would probably have enough knowledge in you to serve many people for a generation."

He was then quick to say, "I'm not saying you shouldn't study the Bible. Don't you walk outta here and say, 'Sy doesn't honor the Word and believe in studying.'"

I'm right there with him. The point is we so often use lack of knowledge as an excuse to put off being who we need to be.

I've done this. In fact, I keep falling into this trap: I put off actually *doing* the stuff to *study* the stuff. Instead of writing this book, for instance, I'm constantly tempted to read more about writing books.

Yes, any follower of Jesus will want to learn about him. Any hockey player will want to learn more about the game. But learning is not playing the actual game.

Paul writes to the believers in Rome, "I myself am convinced, my brothers and sisters, that you yourselves are full of goodness, filled with knowledge and competent to instruct one another" (Rom. 15:14). Seriously? "Filled with knowledge"? They were a group of new believers. They had exactly zero (0) Christian colleges. No seminaries. No awesome, inspiring books like this one.

> **Learning is not playing the actual game.**

They didn't even have Bibles.

But Paul is telling them, "You know enough to do this."

It's true that you can study the wonders of God for the rest of your life and never run out of new and exciting discoveries. It's a wonderful part of life with God. And Jesus was clearly committed to memorizing Scripture. He quoted it constantly. These are very good things.

But the game starts now.

Playing the game is putting what Jesus told us to do into practice: Loving our enemies. Praying for people who persecute us. Forgiving people as we've been forgiven. Blessing those who curse us. Praying for God's kingdom on earth as it is in heaven. Putting off the tendency to store up things for ourselves and instead being wildly generous.

In Luke 10, an expert in the law asks Jesus what he needs to do to inherit eternal life. Jesus responds with a question: "What is written in the Law?" (v. 26).

The expert quotes Scripture: "'Love the Lord your God with all your heart and with all your soul and with all your strength and with all your mind'; and, 'Love your neighbor as yourself'" (v. 27).

Jesus tells him he's right on. But watch the move the expert makes immediately after: "He wanted to justify himself, so he asked Jesus, 'And who is my neighbor?'" (v. 29).

Suddenly the expert has no idea what "neighbor" means. He'd rather keep this whole thing academic.

Jesus:	Love your enemies.
Religious experts:	Let's maybe study this first.
Jesus:	If you don't forgive, you won't be forgiven.
Religious experts:	Well, he doesn't mean it quite like that. There's a lot of nuance there.
Jesus:	No, I meant that.
Religious experts:	Let's study it.
Jesus:	No, I just want you to do it.
Religious experts:	What does "do" mean, really? In Aramaic?
Jesus:	What in the world.

It reminds me of when I had an epiphany on a basketball court in middle school. During our PE class, we'd get a chance to shoot around, and inevitably, I would take (and miss) inventive trick shots. I'd do shots from behind the backboard, half-court hook shots, and so forth, until it suddenly dawned on me, *I can't shoot free throws. I'm not even solid on layups. Why am I doing trick shots when I can't make normal shots?*

Wait. Maybe it's because *I can't make normal shots.*

I think a lot of our intellectual lives can operate that way. Maybe we prefer debating ideas to actually doing the stuff. Maybe people like me enjoy making the stuff more complex than it needs to be so we can keep avoiding it.

Yet I love how quickly non-expert types in the Gospels and in Acts can go from being relatively uneducated to full-throttle followers of Jesus. They just start following him. They start as his apprentices. That's the best way to learn, it turns out.

> **Don't let others convince you you're not enough, you don't know enough, or you don't have the expertise. You can do this today.**

Make no mistake, following Jesus means *doing the stuff*. Even if you're not steeped in religious training or you're absolutely brand-new to living a Jesus-shaped life, you can start doing it right now. You don't need to wait until you've reached some level of mastery over all the information.

Don't let others convince you you're not enough, you don't know enough, or you don't have the expertise. You can do this today.

We need you to take the field.

The Dangerous Myth
of "As Long As I'm Not
Hurting Someone Else . . ."

Here's a popular way to evaluate our own behavior: "As long as what I'm doing doesn't hurt someone else, it's okay." It seems nonjudgmental. It's easy to remember. It's simple. There's a lot to like about it. But let's talk more about it.

"As long as I don't hurt anyone else" is so simple. It's simplistic, even. So simplistic, in fact, that it's a lie. It pretends that we can act completely independent of each other, as autonomous, detached selves in a disconnected world of individuals.

But nothing we do is truly private. What we do and who we are have consequences that ripple outward, whether we like it or not. What's more, what we *don't* do and who we *aren't* also have consequences.

I'll use my friend Greg as an example. He's one of my favorite people. He has a strong personality, and he'd tell you that he can be hard to take sometimes, but I don't think so. He says he has average intelligence, but he's an intelligent guy.

I always enjoy hanging out with him. We laugh a lot. He's brutally and refreshingly honest. He's also a guy's guy who hunts and fishes and has a big truck. I just bought a used Honda Fit. But somehow we're friends.

Because he's about my age, he also grew up in an era of video games and easily accessed pornography. At some point in his college years, he could have said, "You know what? I'm going to hole up in my room and collapse inwardly. I'm going to just play and amuse myself. As long as I'm not hurting someone else, what does it matter?"

Thankfully, he didn't do that. Instead, he rose to the occasion and finished college. He then got into medical school (he says he still doesn't know how he made it) and worked very hard. He's now a pediatric cardiac anesthesiologist.

Greg is remarkably good at putting scared little kids to sleep and putting their parents at ease too. He has five kids of his own and a wife who respects him deeply. Because of his desire to emulate Jesus, he's spent months traveling through developing nations (often taking his family), serving in hospitals for the poorest people in the world. He's provided first-class care to some of the most desperate little patients in the world and trained more doctors to do the same.

His field is tricky, and there are horrific consequences when the work is done poorly. There's no doubt his dedication and his willingness to be a keeper of the garden have saved the lives of the vulnerable.

So, the obvious question: If he had, in fact, collapsed inwardly and handed himself over to video games and porn, would it have "hurt" anyone?

Of course, but he wouldn't have known it. We would have missed out on the man he was supposed to be.

This is not an exaggeration. Because of the choices Greg has made, many moms and dads haven't had to attend funerals for their own children.

When we men take our roles seriously, when we're at our best, those are the kinds of things that happen. Healing. Peace. Life.

And when we don't, distortion, anxiety, violence, and meaninglessness fill the gap.

No one operates in a vacuum. There is no such thing as private sin. And there is no such thing as private virtue. Who you are reverberates through your home and neighborhood and the world.

Once, another friend of mine—we'll call him Bob—did something really, really bad. Not illegal, but bad enough that even two years later, it showed up in the headlines of a major metro newspaper, a thousand miles away from where he did it.

I love Bob. He's fun, smart, and fairly new to Christian belief. He accepted responsibility for what he did, and he had to live with it every day.

> If he had, in fact, collapsed inwardly and handed himself over to video games and porn, would it have "hurt" anyone? Of course, but he wouldn't have known it.

He told me after the news resurfaced that he was sorry even I was now having to deal with it. "I'm amazed how many people this has affected," he said. "One stupid, wrong decision I made and it keeps affecting so many people. My wife, my kids . . . it just keeps going."

And so it does.

We marveled at that and just stood there quietly, shaking our heads. Amazing? Yes. But not really surprising.

Our sins don't all wind up in the headlines, but the surface of the pond is never undisturbed by the pebble. The ripples move well beyond ourselves, and in many cases, they radiate through generations. So many people, so many stories, changed because of our decisions.

Even the sins in our head aren't private. Mine affect my attitude. They keep me from being concerned about other people. They make me a jerk in seemingly unrelated ways. ("Why's Brant being a jerk?" "Probably something seemingly unrelated.")

Turns out few things have done more harm than the as-long-as-I-do-no-harm ethic. The as-long-as-I'm-not-hurting-someone-else construct of morality is built atop the swamp of affluence. We afford this lie because affluence loves not only privacy but the fantasy of privacy—the illusion that we can exist as entirely independent creatures.

When I throw myself into what 1 John 2:16 calls "the lust of the flesh, the lust of the eyes, and the pride of life," it saps my energy. And then I'm not the person I'm supposed to be. I'm less creative. I'm less joyful. I have less social energy. My patience is gone. I care less about my neighbors.

Private rebellion. Public consequences. And if it seems unfair that what my friend did was so horrible but what you or I do in our minds is somehow not so horrible, then you agree with Jesus. There *is* no difference.

We need you to be the man you are made to be. Make no mistake, there is no "as long as I'm not hurting someone else . . ."

If you're not who you're made to be, it hurts you.

And it hurts us.

People with Self-Control Are More Interesting

For some reason, a self-controlled person is considered boring.

And maybe they are, as long as by "boring" we mean successful, influential, respected, and admired. Very few people who become those things do so without a great degree of self-control, at least in the areas in which they've become respected or successful.

Michael Jordan punched his teammates. So he lacked self-control in that sense, but he's not in the Hall of Fame of Pals. He's in the Basketball Hall of Fame, because of his repeated willingness to practice when he didn't feel like it. To force himself to use his left hand when it was his weakness. To take thousands of jump shots in front of no one when he knew he wasn't a pure shooter.

Doing things when you don't feel like it, in the service of a higher mission, demonstrates self-control.

If you have a grandfather you admire, I'm confident you don't admire him for his *lack* of self-control. It's because he did something respectable, and that thing is the result of his repeated willingness to do what needed to be done, regardless of how he felt in the moment.

Self-control is simply self-governing. It's deciding, "This is important to do!" and then being able to do it.

Ironic, maybe: The letters I'm typing right now are the result of self-control. Writing is very hard work for me. I try to avoid it. When I need to write, it's amazing how productive I become—at other stuff. I'm suddenly outside replanting flowers I've never cared about, reorganizing my shelf of robots, or going full Dave Ramsey on our previously neglected finances. All of a sudden I'm Mr. Productivity when it comes to everything . . . except the thing I most need to be doing.

But I'm an adult. I can't merely follow my impulses or I'll never get anything done. I have a mission in life: I want to serve people and hopefully speak wisdom into their lives. I can't accomplish this if I'm following my immediate feelings. So here I am.

When we do stupid, immature, destructive things—things we *know* are destructive—we'll want to make excuses for ourselves. We'll want to spin reality and avoid the central problem, which is us. We'll want to say, "I couldn't help it!" And it sounds convincing to us, as long as we don't think about it too much.

But we can help it. Of course we can. We should at least own that instead of lying to ourselves and others.

Let's take the classic, almost universal temptation of pornography with the "I couldn't help it!" excuse. What if someone was willing to give you ten million dollars to make it through one week without porn? And if you failed, you would lose an eye. Could you help it then?

Or what if you were on camera 24/7 and your mom or wife or girlfriend or best friends were watching? Would you be able to "help it"?

> While our will can be very weak in the moment, what we surround ourselves with can make a big difference.

Yes, these are ridiculous scenarios. No one is going to offer you ten million dollars for this. Probably. Or take your eye. Probably. Unless it's some new reality show, which I totally might pitch to somebody now that I think of it. But that's not the point. The point is that while our will can be very weak in the moment, what we surround ourselves with can make a big difference.

This morning I left my house to go write at a coffee shop. Why? Because I know from experience that if I stay home, I'll get distracted and suddenly "feel" that I need to take more breaks and wind up playing FIFA on the PlayStation. I won't get my writing done.

So here's how to attack our self-control problem:

1. *Expand the vision for who you are and who we need you to be.*

You're actually doing that by reading this book. Hopefully you're seeing what it looks like to be a man after God's own heart, a keeper of his garden. Hopefully you're getting a vision for yourself as a man who is a blessing to his community, a defender and protector of the vulnerable.

In the end, I don't want to look back on my life and think of all the video games I played or the fake things I consumed. I do want to look back and see that I tended my garden well, that people around me flourished because I knew my role. I did virtuous, good things, even when I didn't feel like it.

2. *In light of that vision, use your self-control to change circumstances.*

Desperate people are willing to do that, I've noticed. People whose self-control has failed them to the point of destruction with alcohol often avoid their old bars and hangouts. They know the circumstances wherein their self-control is especially weak, and they make decisions beforehand to avoid those situations.

I had a friend who was married and often traveled and stayed in hotels for long periods of time. He would ask the hotel staff to remove the TV before he got there (this was back around 2000, before most of us had laptops or smartphones). He knew if he made that decision ahead of time, his weak self-control wouldn't have to battle with the allure of porn or the wasted time of watching TV. He could stay focused on getting his work done and serve his larger vision of being an honorable husband and father who was growing up in spiritual maturity, rather than stunting his own growth.

Again, our will is not particularly strong. But we can use what we have to recognize patterns of weakness and find other ways to live. We can start to see the problems coming. We can change circumstances.

3. *Be around people more.*

I'm an introvert, but I know it's not good to be alone. I need people.

You may be too young to remember this, but practically every TV action show back in the 70s to 90s wrapped up at the bar or the group hangout. The good guys would be relaxing after everything was resolved, and they'd joke about something, start laughing, and maybe lift a beer, and then . . . the frame would freeze. Credits would roll.

It was such a cliché that one show, *Police Squad*, brilliantly mocked it. While the characters would freeze and credits would roll, there'd be one guy in the group who, for some reason, didn't freeze. And when he realized everyone else was oddly frozen, he'd start grabbing their wallets and keys.

Anyway, I've realized I've always kind of yearned for that. Not the freezing part, but the pure joy of having a challenge in front of me and some comrades. We work hard, accomplish the thing—a good thing—and then have a big, fun dinner or something.

This has happened a few times, and there's something deeply satisfying about it. We're all tired but ready to laugh and enjoy each other's company. It's like being back at the Shire after the whole Mordor thing.

It's amazing how we don't feel as tempted at times like that. Again, I could adapt to hermithood pretty easily, but I know now that's how I'll collapse inward. My judgment will be distorted. I won't be who I need to be for others.

We've got to be around people. There's only so much free time we need. We need projects and mission and community. That's when we thrive. Many of our seemingly inescapable, ever-present temptations become escapable and not always present when we are doing things with people.

So much of self-control is about changing our circumstances, what's on our daily schedules, and the people we are around.

> So much of self-control is about changing our circumstances, what's on our daily schedules, and the people we are around.

If you yearn for a change of circumstances but you're not sure how to make it happen, I highly recommend asking God repeatedly for it. I'm confident it's something he wants for you too. I'm convinced he'll help us with it if we ask.

So let's ask.

Boldly Ask God—
Sarcastically, If Necessary

Speaking of asking . . . I'm not proud of this story.

It's strange. I'm simultaneously a little ashamed of it and elated by it.

Here's what happened. I was out running on a sunny day. I was doing something I rarely did at the time: I was praying out loud. And I was praying sarcastically, which is also odd.

Now, you should know that at the time, my wife and I had two little kids, and we could only afford one car. I was hosting a radio morning show, so I needed to be at work very early in the morning. We didn't like doing it, but since we only had one car, my wife would give me a ride to work and we'd have to leave the kids alone for a bit while they slept. We weren't quite sure what to do about the situation.

So I was out running and talking to God. Again, this was out loud: "Could you please give us a car?"

I looked to my left, where a man was driving a Jeep Wrangler with the top removed. He looked super cool riding around with his little boy, about my son's age, in the Florida sun.

"And while you're at it, can you make it a convertible?" I actually said those words. To God. Again, it was sarcastic. I was making fun of myself for asking.

Whenever I tell people this story, I have to let them know that my theology doesn't really allow for this sort of request—"God, I want this thing"—like he's some kind of vending machine. The free convertible request was my ironic sense of humor. I don't usually pray that kind of prayer, and I don't think it's a mature prayer, and I would never advise someone to start praying like that.

. . . But someone gave me a convertible before the end of the day. Out of nowhere.

I'm not kidding. That actually happened.

Carolyn and I were newly part of a small Bible study for parents, just four youngish couples, who met in a room in a church building. We barely knew the others. That very evening, a few hours after my jog, one of the guys in the group, a lawyer named Luke, told me he had a weird thing happen: His in-laws had given a minivan to his family. They were glad to have it.

Then Luke said he felt like God wanted him to give me his car. It's not something we'd talked about before, but they didn't need three vehicles. Did we need a vehicle, by chance? And if we did, would I be okay driving a convertible?

Why, yes, I would be okay driving a convertible.

I was in disbelief at what was happening.

Luke drove me to his house while Carolyn headed home to relieve our babysitter. Luke got his stuff out of the trunk and glove compartment. I'm not sure I could have said anything. I think my mouth was hanging open.

The car was an Infiniti with 50,000 miles. "It runs great," he said, and he signed over his title. Within minutes I was driving with the top down through the warm night air. I couldn't believe it.

(I *still* can't believe it. I mean, what are the odds, absent God's involvement in this?)

I arrived at home and went upstairs, where the kids were in their bunk beds. They hadn't quite gone to sleep.

"Hey Justice, hey Julia . . . I want to tell you a story." Stories got immediate attention, especially when they weren't expecting one. "You know how we need a car, right?"

I told them I'd prayed for help. I'd actually asked God for a convertible. Out loud I'd asked him this. Today.

"And now I want you to come downstairs!"

They followed after me in their pajamas. Carolyn and I put them in the convertible, and we went for a ride under the stars. It's a night they haven't forgotten, and I certainly never will either.

Two takeaways from Brant's free convertible story:

1. This whole thing was against my theology.
2. My theology is often stupid.

Why is it stupid? Because God isn't a math equation. He refuses to be pinned down so easily. He will not be controlled, figured out, or reduced to the if-then predictability of binary code.

Does God answer sarcastic prayers? Of course not.

Except when he does.

Does God give out free convertibles? Of course not.

Except when he does.

Here's a takeaway you shouldn't take away, but I'll bet your mind went there: "Okay, so I'll sarcastically ask God for an awesome vehicle because apparently it works."

But "it" doesn't work. God does what he wants. Our attempt to make "it" work is, essentially, reducing prayer to a magic spell. ("If I say such-and-such just so, this will happen!")

Actual relationships don't work that way. If, as a dad, I did something wonderful to surprise my daughter by meeting a need in a delightful way, I would be alarmed if she tried to repeat her actions in order to make "it" happen again.

There is no "it." There is only a "he," and he wants us to relate to him with honesty and passion. Like this relationship really matters. Like he is listening and actually loves us.

I mentioned that I'm a bit ashamed of this story, and it's true. But that's a selfish thing, this shame.

I'm ashamed because I feel silly. I did nothing to earn a car, and it's such a seemingly childish story. It doesn't fit my normal idiom. It doesn't make me seem respectable.

But who cares about my idiom? This story happened, and mostly I think it's wonderful and funny.

Sometimes when I read about God's interactions with people in Scripture, I see unpredictability. One minute he's speaking through a burning bush. The next he's speaking through an old man. Then a king. Then a donkey.

> **Sometimes when I read about God's interactions with people in Scripture, I see unpredictability. One minute he's speaking through a burning bush. The next he's speaking through an old man. Then a king. Then a donkey.**

I've learned to talk to him honestly. Brutally honestly. Out loud. I encourage you to do this too. It's central to taking responsibility for your own spiritual life. Ask not just because he gives us stuff but because of two things:

1. God loves you. And because of that, he'll do things.
2. If you don't ask, who will?

CONCLUSION

A Final Word about Adam . . . and Us

We started with him. We'll end with him.

We talked about how Adam blew it. He was given a job, and he failed.

I can relate to the failure part. I presume you can too.

But you know what? There's more to the story.

Adam isn't just in the beginning of the Old Testament. He shows up at the beginning of the New Testament too.

He's in Luke 3, in the genealogy of Jesus (which I've always kind of skipped over, honestly). I'm going to include the whole thing here, all seventy-seven generations, because I want you to see exactly how Adam, the man who failed, is described.

> Now Jesus himself was about thirty years old when he
> began his ministry. He was the son, so it was thought,
> of Joseph,
> the son of Heli, the son of Matthat,
> the son of Levi, the son of Melki,
> the son of Jannai, the son of Joseph,
> the son of Mattathias, the son of Amos,
> the son of Nahum, the son of Esli,
> the son of Naggai, the son of Maath,
> the son of Mattathias, the son of Semein,
> the son of Josek, the son of Joda,

the son of Joanan, the son of Rhesa,
the son of Zerubbabel, the son of Shealtiel,
the son of Neri, the son of Melki,
the son of Addi, the son of Cosam,
the son of Elmadam, the son of Er,
the son of Joshua, the son of Eliezer,
the son of Jorim, the son of Matthat,
the son of Levi, the son of Simeon,
the son of Judah, the son of Joseph,
the son of Jonam, the son of Eliakim,
the son of Melea, the son of Menna,
the son of Mattatha, the son of Nathan,
the son of David, the son of Jesse,
the son of Obed, the son of Boaz,
the son of Salmon, the son of Nahshon,
the son of Amminadab, the son of Ram,
the son of Hezron, the son of Perez,
the son of Judah, the son of Jacob,
the son of Isaac, the son of Abraham,
the son of Terah, the son of Nahor,
the son of Serug, the son of Reu,
the son of Peleg, the son of Eber,
the son of Shelah, the son of Cainan,
the son of Arphaxad, the son of Shem,
the son of Noah, the son of Lamech,
the son of Methuselah, the son of Enoch,
the son of Jared, the son of Mahalalel,
the son of Kenan, the son of Enosh,
the son of Seth, the son of *Adam*,
the son of God. (Luke 3:23–38, italics mine)

I hope what I've written in this book is life-giving wisdom for you. I'm still learning, of course. One thing I'm continuing to learn is that God loves me when I don't live up to my own standards, my own vision for who I need to be. I know I'm growing up. But the failures can haunt me.

And yet . . . there's Adam again. *God's son. Still.*

Sometimes the Christian story can be confusing. I can find myself wondering all over again, *Why would God do what he did for us? Why the cross? Why would he do that?*

And then I see Adam on this list. "The son of God."

God didn't make that sacrifice for just any reason. No one does that. No, we only make that kind of sacrifice for family.

We are called to do Adam's job. We're keepers of the garden, protectors and defenders and coworkers in the kingdom of God. All these things I've asked you to consider in this book—obviously, I think they're vital for us and those around us.

But if you are also like Adam in that you've failed (and you have, and so have I), please take note of this: If there's an epitaph for Adam, and for you and me, it remains "a son of God."

God still claims us. Still wants us.

Think about that. He knows us better than we know ourselves. We see ourselves in terms of our accomplishments, our résumés, our successes, our failures, and the roles we are currently filling. We see ourselves in terms of what we look like or how people react to us. We can't even see the real, stripped-down, raw us.

But he does. He knows it all. And he's not walking away.

Imagine that.

No one else can see us like that. No one else can love us like that. That's a strong place to be.

Knowing that, we can journey from here. Be a blessing to the women and children around you—and other guys, while you're at it. Add value to their lives. Give them a glimpse of a man who knows who he is and whose he is.

A guy like that isn't afraid. He laughs a lot. He knows how it ends, and he knows that despite our mistakes, God is planning to make all things new.

And just as God described the beginning, the end—for those who want him—will be very, very good.

DISCUSSION QUESTIONS

Keeper of the Garden

1. When you first hear the phrase "a real man," what images come to mind? What does this man look like? What does he do for a living? What kind of vehicle does he drive? What does he wear, eat, and so on?

2. Brant points back to Adam and says that the purpose of man is to be the "keeper of the garden." Describe in your own words what this title implies.

3. If you were forced to play one video game eight hours a day for thirty days, what game would it be and why? (Brant's answer is clearly FIFA.) More importantly, what did you think of "Jake" and the idea that a man can do whatever he wants as long as he's not hurting anyone else? Is that even possible? Why or why not?

4. Discuss your response to the following ideas:

   A. Masculinity is about taking responsibility.

   B. Women see rescuing as attractive.

   C. Nobody admires a passive man.

   D. The scariest thing should be that you might never become the man you were intended to be.

Decision One: Forsake the Fake and Relish the Real

1. Brant comments that sin is a swindle: "There's this sweet taste—at first. Then there's a dark turn, and we're left with bitterness and pain. That's how sin works. Always promising, initially exciting, this rush of freedom . . . and then the punch in the gut." Have you experienced this? In what way?

2. "Lust is the craving for salt of a man who is dying of thirst." Explain this statement. How does it relate to you?

3. What's dangerous about "supernormal stimuli"?

4. Discuss your response to this statement: "Please don't waste your God-given desire for adventure and accomplishment by being a fake hero fighting fake injustices in fake worlds." Is Brant right that this can be a problem? If so, how?

5. Brant writes that if we give up our addictions, we must have a bigger vision for our lives. If you were to write a mission statement for the man you want to be, what would it look like?

Decision Two: Protect the Vulnerable

1. The word "vulnerable" is used often in this book, and for good reason. What does it mean, and who are the vulnerable people around you?

2. What, if anything, was surprising to you about the outcomes of the Mouse Utopia experiments?

3. "What you do actually matters," Brant writes. Do you agree that there are some things that will happen only if *you* actively do something? Why or why not?

4. In what ways does our culture influence us to betray our role as protectors and keepers of the garden?

5. The people in our home should feel more secure because we're there. Did you have that security from your father growing up, or was he absent or threatening? How might you do things differently?

6. Why does Brant not object to the "sheltering" of children? How does the media in particular affect kids, and what is your role in making sure their childhood doesn't end prematurely?

Decision Three: Be Ambitious about the Right Things

1. If you are ambitious about the wrong things, you will be hit by reality eventually. Name two or three regrets, things you wish you could go back and change because you were ambitious about the wrong things. How have those regrets ended up affecting your life and those around you?

2. Brant says that even terrible jobs make us serve people. What meaning does your work have to you? How does it make you serve people?

3. "Contentment brings freedom. Discontentment makes you dependent." Explain what this statement means.

4. Psalm 23:1 says, "The Lord is my Shepherd, I lack nothing." Is that believable to you—that you can lack nothing? How might really believing that make life as a man better?

5. "Commitment means closing certain doors in favor of opening a better one," Brant writes. What have you given up in order to fulfill the most important roles in your life? What might you still need to give up?

Decision Four: Make Women and Children Feel Safe, Not Threatened

1. How does what Jesus did for the woman caught in adultery stand in stark contrast to how Adam protected—or didn't protect—Eve?

2. Read James 3:5–12. Write or discuss some encouraging things you need to say to the ones closest to you—maybe something that you have never said or don't say enough—and say those things to them as soon as possible.

3. "I came to realize that the man I needed to kill in order to protect my wife is myself as a sinner." What is your response to this statement? Can you relate to the damage you can cause with your anger and harsh words in your own home? In what way?

4. What's your reaction to the story about the man who had a massive platform to help children but ultimately didn't care for his wife and daughters?

5. Why is it crucial to realize that life has seasons?

Decision Five: Choose Today Who You Will Become Tomorrow

1. Who you become is a direct result of what you pay attention to. Standing guard over your mind is vital. Read 2 Corinthians 10:5 and Colossians 3:12–17. What does it mean to take every thought captive to make it obedient to Christ? What practical advice would you give someone who is struggling with their thought life?

2. We should not be defined by our desires, Brant says. How might letting our desires define and rule over us lead to destruction?

3. Do you agree with Larry Crabb that most guys are needy? At the deepest level, what are they needy *for*?

4. We truly have nothing to fear. If God is for us, who can be against us? Read Romans 8:35–39. What words stick out the most and why? How do you feel after reading this passage?

5. Jeremiah 17:9 states, "The heart is deceitful above all things, and desperately sick; who can understand it?"

(ESV). When Brant says, "Don't follow your heart—open your eyes," what does he mean?

Decision Six: Take Responsibility for Your Own Spiritual Life

1. What do you think of Brant's idea that what God is looking for from us is a believing, trusting loyalty?
2. What role do feelings have in your spiritual life? Do you need to feel God's presence or experience "religious feelings" in order to be loyal to him? Why or why not?
3. Many people think they need their anger in order to act. Why is that a flawed idea?
4. "Whatever I do is fine as long as I'm not hurting someone else" is a common, modern idea. Why is it a misleading one?
5. How can changing our schedules help us with self-control problems?
6. What did you think of Brant's car-prayer story? Can you give an example of a brutally honest prayer that you have prayed? Spend some time right now in brutally honest prayer. Ask God to help you be one of the men we need.

Conclusion: A Final Word about Adam . . . and Us

Remember, God still claims us. He still wants us. He can help us change. That's a strong place to be.

1. Why does the inclusion and description of Adam in Jesus' genealogy tell us about how God views us even when we fail?
2. Spend a few minutes (or more) talking about the man you want to be. Describe your vision for who you want to become, how you will treat people, and how you can be a keeper of the garden around you.

ACKNOWLEDGMENTS

Thank you, Carolyn, for thirty-one years of being my friend, believing in me, helping me grow up as a man, and even encouraging me to write this book.

Thank you to the rest of my family, both physical and spiritual, for encouragement, laughs, and prayers: Justice, Julia and Zach, Mom, Smitty, Dad, Miss Bev, Sherri, Aunt Nana, Brendon, Chris, Daniel, Jonny, Jeff, Mike, and Amber.

Special thanks to my brother, Darin, for writing the questions for small group discussion, which he has done so well for my other books. (You can download them all for free at branthansen.com.)

And our awesome neighbors Trish, David, and Emma. I just thought it would be fun to put you in here somewhere. You guys free this evening?

I'd also like to "acknowledge" that I just finished writing a Christian book on masculinity and I never mentioned *Braveheart*. Nothing against the movie; I just wanted to see if I could do it. (Gives self fist-bump.)

Additionally, Aidan Nielsen. I just have this sense that you are going to be a great man, in the best sense of "great." You're going to be a blessing to people. A strong defender and servant. That's gonna be you.

The amazing Dutch Patterson. At this writing, you're fifteen, but please store this book somewhere after reading it and break it out in twenty-five years. Was I right? Are you awesome? I was right. You were already awesome, so I can't give myself too much credit.

And to Jessa Medsker. On Facebook, your mom asked me to put you in my acknowledgments. She said you're only six, but you and I have much in common —we're both on the autism spectrum and you love toast like me. She said your smile lights up the room. She shared a photo, and your smile lit up my room too.

NOTES

Masculinity Is about Taking Responsibility

1. Megan McCluskey, "Gillette Makes Waves with Controversial New Ad Highlighting 'Toxic Masculinity,'" *Time*, January 16, 2019, https://time.com/5503156/gillette-razors-toxic-masculinity.

2. Bible Study Tools, "Shamar," accessed October 5, 2021, https://www.biblestudytools.com/lexicons/hebrew/nas/shamar.html.

The Ancient Art of Blaming Other People

1. James Clear, "3 Ideas, 2 Quotes, 1 Question," November 5, 2020, email newsletter.

The Scariest Thing

1. "Millennial Melancholy: Nine in Ten Young Brits Believe Their Life Lacks Purpose, according to Shocking New Study," *The Sun*, August 2, 2019, https://www.thesun.co.uk/news/9637619/young-brits-life-lacks-purpose.

The Fake Life and Where It Leads

1. "She Is Broken & Being Repaired, Says Kazakh Bodybuilder Who Married His Sex Doll," DNA, December 26, 2020, https://www.dnaindia.com/world/report-she-is-broken-being-repaired-says-kazakh-bodybuilder-who-married-his-sex-doll-2864146.

2. Franki Cookney, "Sex Doll Sales Surge in Quarantine, but It's Not Just about Loneliness," *Forbes*, May 21, 2020, https://www.forbes.com/sites/frankicookney/2020/05/21/sex-doll-sales-surge-in-quarantine-but-its-not-just-about-loneliness.

3. "Our Technology," Robot Companion, accessed August 19, 2021, https://www.robotcompanion.ai/our-technology.

"That's Not a Girl. That's a Piece of Paper."

1. Deirdre Barrett, "Your Mind Is a Victim of Stone Age Instincts," *Wired*, July 5, 2015, https://www.wired.co.uk/article/stone-age-mind.

2. Kurt Vonnegut, *God Bless You, Mr. Rosewater* (New York: Dell, 1965), 109.

3. Susan Weinschenk, "The Dopamine-Seeking Reward Loop," *Psychology Today*, February 28, 2018, https://www.psychologytoday.com/us/blog/brain-wise/201802/the-dopamine-seeking-reward-loop.

4. Bruce Marshall, *The World, the Flesh, and Father Smith* (Boston: Houghton Mifflin, 1945), 114.

5. Frederick Buechner, *Wishful Thinking* (New York: Harper & Row, 1973), 54.

Here's Some Good News about Pornography. No, Really.

1. "How Watching Porn Can Take Away a Guy's Ability to Have Sex in Real Life," Fight the New Drug, August 7, 2018, https://fightthenewdrug.org/porn-is-taking-away-mens-ability-to-have-actual-sex.

2. Dr. Carlo Foresta, "Project AndroLIFE, Health and Sex" (lecture), 2014, https://www.yourbrainonporn.com/porn-induced-sexual-dysfunctions/experts-who-recognize-porn-induced-sexual-dysfunctions-along-with-relevant-studies/pdf-of-a-lecture-by-carlo-foresta-urology-professor-2014.

3. Foresta, "Project AndroLIFE, Health and Sex."

4. Dr. Philip Zimbardo and Nikita Duncan, "The Demise of Guys: How Video Games and Porn Are Ruining a Generation," CNN, May 24, 2012, https://www.cnn.com/2012/05/23/health/living-well/demise-of-guys/index.html.

5. Gary Wilson, "The Great Porn Experiment," TEDx Talks, May 16, 2012, YouTube video, 4:45, https://www.youtube.com/watch?v=wSF82AwSDiU.

6. Wilson, "The Great Porn Experiment," 16:21.

7. K_B, "Day 319, the biggest changes I've experienced so far in my life . . . ," Reddit, February 1, 2021, https://www.reddit.com/r/NoFap/comments/kkk1ub/day_319_the_biggest_changes_ive_experienced_so.

8. dodo_005, "I love you guys, I did it. 90 days completed and today is my birthday. The best birthday gift I gave to myself," Reddit, February 1, 2021, https://www.reddit.com/r/NoFap/comments/kkau8g/i_love_you_guys_i_did_it_90_days_completed_and.

9. NinjaRabbIT09, "Feeling so much better," Reddit, July 1, 2019, https://www.reddit.com/r/NoFap/comments/9pobve/feeling_so_much_better.

10. MiddlewaysOfTruth-2, comment on Startagain2020, "I guess watching porn fills me with hatred," Reddit, February 1, 2021, https://www.reddit.com/r/NoFap/comments/kkgifs/i_guess_watching_porn_fills_us_with_hatred.

11. GiraffePuncher69, "90 days- I did it," Reddit, February 1, 2021, https://www.reddit.com/r/NoFap/comments/kk8w8q/90_days_i_did_it.

A Tale of Two Men, and Every Single Woman

1. The Star, "Malian Hero Scales Paris Building to Save Child," YouTube video, May 28, 2018, https://youtu.be/WISmbOw_bMk.

About Video Games

1. Ishikawa Kiyoshi, "'Hikikomori': Social Recluses in the Shadows of an Aging Japan," Nippon.com, July 19, 2017, https://www.nippon.com/en/currents/d00332.

2. Laurence Butet-Roch, "Pictures Reveal the Isolated Lives of Japan's Recluses," *National Geographic*, February 14, 2018, https://www.nationalgeographic.com/photography/proof/2018/february/japan-hikikomori-isolation-society/#close.

Your Neighborhood Should Be Safer Simply Because You're There

1. Riaan Grobler, "'I Couldn't Imagine Ever Doing Anything Like That'—Man Who Tackled Alleged Restaurant Child Snatcher," News24, September 14, 2020, https://www.news24.com/news24/southafrica/news/i-never-imagined-doing-something-like-this-man-who-tackled-alleged-restaurant-child-snatcher-20200914.

2. Grobler, "'I Couldn't Imagine.'"

3. Office of Juvenile Justice and Delinquency Prevention, "Statistical Briefing Book," 2019, https://www.ojjdp.gov/ojstatbb/crime/ucr.asp?table_in=1.

Lessons from Mouse Utopia

1. Today I Found Out, "That Time a Guy Tried to Build a Utopia for Mice and It All Went to Hell," YouTube video, December 28, 2018, https://www.youtube.com/watch?v=5m7X-1V9nOs.

2. J. R. R. Tolkien, *The Return of the King* (New York: Random House, 1955), 16.

The Ultimate Betrayal

1. "5 Teenagers Save 2 Small Children after Sled Somehow Ends Up in Frigid New Jersey Pond," CBS New York, December 20, 2020, https://newyork.cbslocal.com/2020/12/20/teenagers-save-children-after-sled-goes-into-pond-atlantic-highlands-new-jersey.

Yes, You Should Shelter Your Children

1. *Saturday Night Live*, "Pre-School—*Saturday Night Live*," YouTube video, October 24, 2013, https://youtu.be/IHTaMMyK274.

2. Jean Twenge, "Teenage Depression and Suicide Are Way Up—and So Is Smartphone Use," *Washington Post*, November 19, 2017, https://www.washingtonpost.com/national/health-science/teenage-depression-and-suicide-are-way-up--and-so-is-smart phone-use/2017/11/17/624641ea-ca13-11e7-8321-481fd63f174d_story.html.

How to Be Incredibly Awesome and Somehow Less Attractive to Women

1. Rachel Bowman, "Viral Video Shows Man Jump from Top of Pennybacker Bridge," CBS Austin, November 28, 2020, https://cbsaustin.com/news/local/viral-video-shows-man-jump-from-top-of-pennybacker-bridge.

Allow Yourself to "Lose"

1. CineClips, "If You Ain't First, You're Last," May 2, 2020, YouTube video, 2:05, https://youtu.be/ar1McsRmBOk.

Don't Be Afraid of Commitments—Be Afraid of *Not* Making Commitments

1. Phil Lempert, "The Scoop on Cereals," *Today*, August 17, 2001, https://www.today.com/news/scoop-cereals-wbna4112859.

How to Treat Women: The Bridger Master Class

1. Bri Lamm, "'If Someone Had to Die, I Thought It Should Be Me'—Chris Hemsworth, Hugh Jackman & Chris Evans Praise 6-Year-Old Hero Who Saved Sister from Dog Attack," Faithit, July 16, 2020, https://faithit.com/if-someone-had-to-die-i-thought-it-should-be-me-chris-hemsworth-chris-evans-praise-bridger-save-sister-dog-attack.

Understand What "Love" Is and Isn't

1. Richard Selzer, *Mortal Lessons: Notes on the Art of Surgery* (San Diego: Harcourt Brace, 1996), 46.

Protect Them . . . from You

1. Richard D. Phillips, *The Masculine Mandate* (Sanford, FL: Reformation Trust Publishing, 2010), 118–19.

Attention Is Everything

1. Dallas Willard, *Renovation of the Heart: Putting On the Character of Christ* (Colorado Springs: The Navigators, 2014), 16.
2. Lisa Magloff, "Repetition as an Advertisement Technique," CHRON, February 1, 2019, https://smallbusiness.chron.com/repetition-advertisement-technique-24437.html.

Foolishness = Pain

1. Eva Krockow, "How Many Decisions Do We Make Each Day?," *Psychology Today*, September 27, 2018, https://www.psychologytoday.com/us/blog/stretching -theory/201809/how-many-decisions-do-we-make-each-day.

Walmart Shopping Cart Attack Guy Never Set Out to Be Walmart Shopping Cart Attack Guy

1. Frances Parkinson Keyes, "A Story of Friendly Flags," *Good Housekeeping*, May 1925, 164.
2. C. S. Lewis, *The Great Divorce* (Glasgow, Scotland: HarperCollins, 1946), 72.

We Don't Need More Needy Guys—We Have Enough of Those

1. Larry Crabb, *Men of Courage: God's Call to Move Beyond the Silence of Adam* (Grand Rapids: Zondervan, 2013), 137.
2. David G. Stern, "Heraclitus," *The Monist*, October 1991, 579–604.

What God Is Looking For

1. J. R. R. Tolkien, *The Fellowship of the Ring* (Boston: Houghton Mifflin, 1988), 150.

Brant Hansen uses his media platforms to advocate for the healing work of CURE, a global network of surgical hospitals for children with disabilities in developing nations. He's a syndicated radio host and the author of *Unoffendable*, *Blessed Are the Misfits*, and *The Truth about Us*. In addition to speaking on the subject of *The Men We Need*, he frequently speaks at churches, conferences, and corporations on the topics of forgiveness, faith and the autism spectrum, and the kingdom of God.

Brant is also a musician and occasional stand-up comedian. He and his wife, Carolyn, live in South Florida.

Connect with
BRANT

Visit **BRANTHANSEN.COM**
for Brant's radio show, blog, podcast, and more!

▶ ⊚ 🐦 BrantHansen   f BrantHansenPage

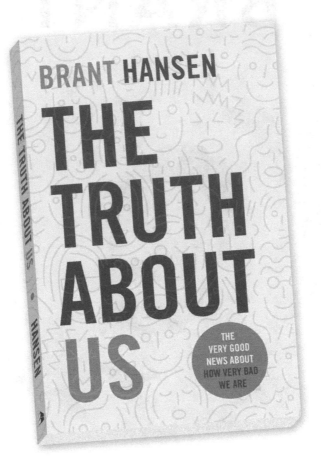

Thank you for reading this book.

I want to leave you with a challenge (and if you can't do it or don't want to do it, that's okay).

Here it is: *Help us heal kids and tell them and their families how much they are loved by God.*

There are millions of kids with disabilities that are correctable. They're subject to abuse and intense rejection. They're often considered cursed. But getting access to surgery changes everything for them.

That's what CURE does! This has been my passion for years. I've visited these hospitals and met these kids, these families, these doctors . . . and this looks like Jesus to me.

Kids can walk and skip and dance and run for the first time in their lives! Moms and dads are crying with joy!

This is what I wish we followers of Jesus were known for: healing. **Please consider jumping online right now (cure.org) and becoming a CURE Hero.**

And if you want some amazing inspiration (and to see where your money is going!), check out this documentary on Amazon Prime or YouTube.

cure

WINNER
GREAT LAKES
CHRISTIAN
FILM FESTIVAL
2018

NOMINEE
INTERNATIONAL
CHRISTIAN
FILM FESTIVAL
2018

WINNER
CHRISTIAN
WORLDVIEW
FILM FESTIVAL
2018

CURE INTERNATIONAL PRESENTS

MODERN DAY
MIRACLES